NEW DIRECTIONS FOR TEACHING AND LEARNING

Robert J. Menges, *Northwestern University*
EDITOR-IN-CHIEF

Marilla D. Svinicki, *University of Texas, Austin*
ASSOCIATE EDITOR

Effective Practices for Improving Teaching

Michael Theall
University of Alabama at Birmingham

Jennifer Franklin
Northeastern University

EDITORS

Number 48, Winter 1991

JOSSEY-BASS INC., PUBLISHERS, San Francisco

MAXWELL MACMILLAN INTERNATIONAL PUBLISHING GROUP
New York • Oxford • Singapore • Sydney • Toronto

EFFECTIVE PRACTICES FOR IMPROVING TEACHING
Michael Theall, Jennifer Franklin (eds.)
New Directions for Teaching and Learning, no. 48
Robert J. Menges, Editor-in-Chief

© 1991 by Jossey-Bass Inc., Publishers. All rights reserved.

No part of this issue may be reproduced in any form—except for a brief quotation (not to exceed 500 words) in a review or professional work—without permission in writing from the publishers.

Microfilm copies of issues and articles are available in 16mm and 35mm, as well as microfiche in 105mm, through University Microfilms Inc., 300 North Zeeb Road, Ann Arbor, Michigan 48106.

LC 85-644763   ISSN 0271-0633   ISBN 1-55542-782-0

NEW DIRECTIONS FOR TEACHING AND LEARNING is part of The Jossey-Bass Higher and Adult Education Series and is published quarterly by Jossey-Bass Inc., Publishers, 350 Sansome Street, San Francisco, California 94104. Second-class postage paid at San Francisco, California, and at additional mailing offices. POSTMASTER: Send address changes to Jossey-Bass Inc., Publishers, 350 Sansome Street, San Francisco, California 94104.

SUBSCRIPTIONS for 1991 cost $45.00 for individuals and $60.00 for institutions, agencies, and libraries.

EDITORIAL CORRESPONDENCE should be sent to Robert J. Menges, Northwestern University, Center for the Teaching Professions, 2003 Sheridan Road, Evanston, Illinois 60208-2610.

Cover photograph by Richard Blair/Color & Light © 1990.

Printed on acid-free paper in the United States of America.

Contents

Editors' Notes 1
Michael Theall, Jennifer Franklin

Part One: The Context of Teaching Improvement

1. The Moment of Truth: Feeding Back Information 7
About Teaching
George L. Geis
Even the most reliable information about teaching is useless if faculty refuse to accept it. What conditions set the stage for faculty acceptance of feedback information and its productive use?

2. The Real World of Teaching Improvement: A Faculty Perspective 21
Robert J. Menges
There are many kinds of information that faculty can use to assess their own performances or those of their peers. Faculty may not perceive all sources of information as equally credible.

3. The Interactions of Teaching Improvement 39
Kathleen T. Brinko
The interpersonal dynamics of teaching improvement have not been thoroughly investigated. What goes on when consultant and client sit down to discuss teaching, and how will knowledge of the interactions of the teaching improvement process lead to more effective teaching?

Part Two: Data for Teaching Improvement

4. Using Assessment Data to Improve Teaching 53
Peter J. Gray
The term *assessment* usually connotes measurement of program or systems effectiveness. But the assessment process can provide data for formative as well as summative purposes.

5. Gathering Data for the Improvement of Teaching: What Do I 65
Need and How Do I Get It?
Karron G. Lewis
There are many ways to collect information about teaching. Many of these methods are quick, easy, and unintrusive and are valuable supplements to the standard source of information: student ratings.

6. Using Student Ratings for Teaching Improvement 83
Michael Theall, Jennifer Franklin
Student ratings systems can be effectively used in teaching improvement efforts. The key is to know what questions to ask and how to analyze, report, and interpret the results.

PART THREE: The Human Resources of Teaching

7. Incorporating Job Satisfaction into a Model of Instructional Effectiveness 99
Patricia Cranton, Robert Knoop
Discussions about teaching and teachers often ignore the fact that faculty are employees of an institution. As such, and particularly because their role embodies the essence of the institution's mission, their job satisfaction should be an important part of these discussions.

8. Quick Starters: New Faculty Who Succeed 111
Robert Boice
Why do some new faculty have high student ratings, the time to do research and writing, and a positive outlook on their careers and their profession? Common characteristics underlie their effectiveness.

9. Report on a Trip Downtown 123
Kenneth O. Doyle
Higher education can learn useful lessons from the business world when it comes to the treatment of faculty as human resources.

INDEX 127

Editors' Notes

The past thirty years have seen many programs, publications, and projects to improve teaching. Suggested methods for improvement have ranged from raising the salaries of faculty, to clinical consultation models, to teaching "great books," to mandated assessment programs. Recently, there has been renewed interest in the "teaching center" model, which saw widespread acceptance and considerable external funding in the late 1960s and early 1970s. Important differences in current approaches to teaching improvement are that teaching center and faculty development resources are now more scarce and that clear evidence of improvement is often required.

Another important facet of this renewed interest in faculty improvement is the visible and tangible support for teaching and learning that has been provided by many college and university presidents. At Miami-Dade Community College, for example, the president initiated the multiyear Teaching-Learning Project. Hallmarks of this project were regular involvement of faculty in achieving consensus on issues and directions, careful and effective communication among all parts of the college system, and the personal involvement of the president in dialogue and shared decision making. Using a different approach, the president of the University of Colorado created the President's Teaching Scholars Program, designed to honor and reward excellence in teaching and scholarship. This program of fostering the relationship between teaching and scholarship has had positive results in both areas.

The views of those who offer teaching improvement programs and services have also changed. Emphasis on models and activities has been supplemented by an interest in the particulars of the contexts and the practices of teaching improvement. This interest has resulted in attempts to define and understand the conditions, interactions, information, and effects of teaching improvement efforts on faculty as individuals as well as on their teaching performance.

This volume, *Effective Practices for Improving Teaching*, focuses on the current thinking and the day-to-day activities of those involved in teaching improvement efforts, whether they are in faculty, teaching consultant, administrator, or multiple roles. The objective of the volume is to provide guidelines for effective practice within the framework of an approach to teaching improvement that considers situational, informational, and per-

---

Contributors to this volume are members of the Special Interest Group in Faculty Evaluation and Development (SIGFED) of the American Educational Research Association. SIGFED actively supports scholarship and the dissemination of information on issues related to faculty evaluation and development.

sonal factors as well as the practical need to collect, analyze, and report data. While the latter activities are necessary for producing reports of results, the former considerations are necessary for understanding the variety and subtleties of teaching, and for giving teaching improvement activities their best chance of success.

This volume is divided into three main parts. Part One deals with the proper conditions for effective feedback, the perceptions of faculty with respect to the value and usefulness of feedback information, and the nature and extent of the interactions between those who provide feedback and those who receive it. In Chapter One, George L. Geis reviews the conditions required for feedback to be effective and accepted. A communications model introduces the discussion, and five components of the feedback process are reviewed: context, sender, message, recipient, and immediate environment. Geis explores the consequences of providing feedback when various aspects of these components fluctuate; he closes the chapter by summarizing the material in a set of guidelines that "put it all together." In Chapter Two, Robert J. Menges develops the argument that effective faculty development requires a view of teaching wrought from the faculty's perspective. This perspective is explored, first, through consideration of faculty beliefs about teaching and "professors' natural inclination to seek feedback." Programmatic implications for improving the information fed back to teachers, reviewing standards, and enhancing teaching repertoires are then reviewed. Finally, Menges proposes a "faculty-centered evaluation and development" approach that incorporates feedback, reflection on standards, and skills learning. Kathleen T. Brinko, in Chapter Three, deals with some of the specifics of consultant-client interactions. She reviews instructional consultation models and relates these to current principles and practices of consultation. She specifies the roles involved in and the nature and extent of the interactions between faculty and teaching improvement specialists, and she identifies similarities and differences based on the experiences and backgrounds of both groups. She then synthesizes this information to provide guidelines for improving consultation and teaching improvement practices at this personal, one-to-one level.

Part Two deals with information needs from a general view (using the assessment metaphor), from a practical, operational view (concerning the kinds of data that can inform improvement), and from a specific, quantitative perspective (focusing on student ratings and their interpretation and use). In Chapter Four, Peter J. Gray examines how the assessment model can be used to guide the ways in which we gather information for teaching improvement. The chapter is general in nature. That is, it does not present lists of techniques or specifics of practice but rather concentrates on the theoretical and practical implications of asking, "What have we learned from the assessment movement that can inform or guide teaching improvement practice?" In Chapter Five, Karron G. Lewis reviews a range of activities and methods for gathering information usable in teaching improvement practice. She focuses on how and why the methods described are useful for teaching improvement and how their results can best be used. Guidelines for choosing methods and suggestions for interpreting and using results are included, along with a "matrix of data needs and sources," a useful tool for planning data collection and for organizing information that can be used to improve teaching. As recent literature has shown over and over, student ratings are the most used and the most misused kind of teaching evaluation data. This misuse occurs not only when ratings are employed in personnel decisions but also when ratings are collected, analyzed, and used for confidential teaching improvement purposes. In Chapter Six, Michael Theall and Jennifer Franklin focus on the tasks of effectively using student ratings instruments and procedures in teaching improvement, reporting ratings data in usable ways for this purpose, and interpreting ratings results.

Part Three deals with the more personal, human side of teaching and addresses such issues as the job satisfaction of faculty and its effects on their teaching, the lessons learned about faculty "burnout" and how it can be avoided, and the ways in which higher education institutions can better treat their human resources. In Chapter Seven, Patricia Cranton and Robert Knoop describe a model of instructional effectiveness that is unique in its inclusion of job satisfaction, both as a concept relevant to understanding the teacher's role and as a secondary measure of the outcomes of teaching. The authors acknowledge that "instructional effectiveness is deeply embedded in the overall college environment and is both responsive to and affected by it." They suggest further research to validate the model so that it will be useful to faculty, administrators, and instructional developers alike. In Chapter Eight, Robert Boice reviews his observational studies at three campuses. The studies investigated how and why some new faculty succeed while others fail, and Boice has drawn several practical conclusions from his work. He contrasts the characteristics of "quick starters" to the behavior of new faculty who encounter problems and often burn out. Boice then summarizes steps that can be taken to assist new faculty who are experiencing difficulty and to capitalize on the strengths of those who are quick starters. He concludes with guidelines designed to assist those who wish to translate these steps into projects suitable to their own campuses' unique cultures and needs. Finally, in Chapter Nine, Kenneth O. Doyle poses the question, "What on earth can we academics learn from business people about how to evaluate and improve college teaching?" Doyle says that he has learned a lot and draws from his experience as a consultant to business in areas of financial management, pension plans, employee benefits, and insurance. He contrasts practices in business with those in higher education and points out how the ways in which business deals with employees have direct application to the treatment of human resources in higher education, in particular to faculty evaluation, development, and improvement.

Michael Theall
Jennifer Franklin
Editors

Michael Theall is associate professor and director of the Teaching and Learning Center at the School of Education, University of Alabama, Birmingham.

Jennifer Franklin is associate director for evaluation and senior research associate in the Office of Instructional Research and Evaluation of the Center for Applied Social Research at Northeastern University, Boston, Massachusetts.

PART ONE

The Context of
Teaching Improvement

The moment of truth comes when evaluative information about teaching is presented to the instructor. The question is, "How can we seize the moment?"

The Moment of Truth: Feeding Back Information About Teaching

George L. Geis

The word *feedback* is associated with the field of cybernetics (Wiener, 1948), but the concept is derived, in good part, from physiology (Cannon, 1932), where it denotes self-regulating systems of a living body. It refers to a process by which information about the effect of a system is fed back into that system, providing potential for adjustment. Thus, a thermostat responds to the temperature of a room, signaling the furnace or air conditioner to operate when the temperature reaches a prespecified point. Now, what does this concept mean for teaching? It presents us with a model and a vocabulary to describe the way in which we provide information to teachers about their teaching.

Typically, the information is gathered as part of an evaluation process, and the feedback can be of various sorts. For example, it can be a pure reflection, such as a film of a teaching episode, or it can be information in some translated form, such as student ratings of a class. It can involve correction, as when the correct answer is given in a programmed text, and it can include some form of guidance, "information provided to instructors that includes recommendations for future improvement" (Gil, 1987, p. 58), as, for example, when a consultant suggests certain actions that can change the impact of instruction. Feedback can refer to the performance itself or to its outcome or impact, that is, we may be looking at either the process of classroom teaching or at examination scores or graduate placements. It may refer to events early in a chain of activities (for example, comments on a course outline) or late in the chain (for example, the quality of term papers). It can be so frequent as to seem continuous, as when we watch the face of a listener as we talk, or it can be given infrequently, like the results of an annual medical checkup. In this chapter, we focus on feedback that involves purposeful, planned collection of information, given at a discontinuous frequency and aimed at improving performance and enhancing the impact of the instructor.

Feedback is often illustrated by a communications model such as shown in Figure 1.1. This is a simple and tempting format for some kinds of analysis, but it does not do justice to the phenomenon that we are exploring here.

If we think of feedback as an information system, then the model in Figure 1.1 suffices; but if an evaluation effort is part of a change process (that is, if we collect information with a goal of improvement), then a more complex model must be used. What interests us is not merely the communication of information but also the change that occurs as a result. Figure 1.2 provides a more complete model for discussion. The whole feedback process occurs in a larger context that can affect any of the elements or interactions of the system. The model emphasizes that feedback has the potential for change, but that a host of conditions must obtain if that potential is to be realized.

The Context

As stressed repeatedly in this chapter, feedback activity, no matter how well carried out, cannot overcome either deficiencies in the organization evaluated or faults in the evaluation process. Before any evaluation is undertaken, sufficient time should be spent on front-end analysis to determine strengths and weaknesses in the larger system. The context includes the degree of clarity of the purposes. Confusion reigns when the stated purposes of evaluation are said to be both formative and summative. We are assuming in this chapter that the purpose of the evaluation is formative and that feedback is given to the professor for purposes of teaching improvement.

Figure 1.1. A Communications Model

SENDER (MESSENGER)—MESSAGE—RECIPIENT

Figure 1.2. A Model for Instructional Feedback

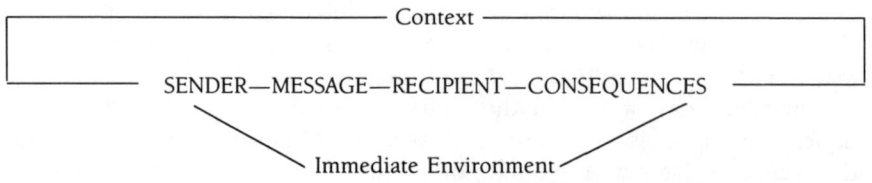

If the purposes are clearly formative, feedback should be linked to a set of resources such as consultation with another person, say, a peer or a faculty developer. The atmosphere may be one of cooperation and trust, or it may be just the opposite. That area is reflected in the feedback activity. The whole effort may be seen as valuable, or it may be considered trivial by members of the campus community.

The Sender

The question of who should provide the information suggests two different things: the source and the messenger. Every source of information is open to criticism. However, the legitimacy of the source can be enhanced by technically sound evaluation procedures and by reference to research, which indicates the degree to which particular sources of data are valid. There appears to be general agreement among evaluators, as well as a hint of agreement among professors, that several sources of data are more impressive than one source (Ory and Braskamp, 1981). In other words, validation from different data sources lends strength to any one set of data.

Senders can be peers who are used to discuss and interpret evaluation results (see Fuhrman and Grasha, 1983), although Centra (1987) suggests that they may be uncomfortable involving themselves in what can be a sensitive procedure. A chairperson, by contrast, may wish to serve as a conduit and may be able to walk the tightrope between being a facilitator and being a supervisor (Seldin and Associates, 1990). Bergquist and Phillips (1975) have suggested that team teaching is an excellent occasion for a continuous exchange of information about teaching and the curriculum.

Students can directly discuss findings with their professors. Such a procedure may be threatening to professors and students alike, yet arrangements can be made to reduce the threat (for example, through the process described by Clark and Beckey, 1979). Of course, one can be one's own informant. Not only can teachers engage in self-rating and reflection, some may even obtain information directly through class debriefings or informal chats with students. Development as an independent self-evaluator may well be one goal of evaluation and feedback.

There are faculty developers or consultants on many campuses today, and they are the most likely messengers when the feedback information is to be combined with support and suggestions that can lead to change. The scant research on the effects that different messengers have on the impact of feedback suggests that the position or role of the messenger (student or supervisor) may influence the message (Tuckman and Oliver, 1968). As the messenger takes on a role somewhat comparable to that of a counselor, he or she should be aware of the literature in related areas. According to Bergquist and Phillips (1975, p. 186), "Interpersonal skills training for the individual who is offering feedback is valuable . . . if not essential." In the literature of higher education, several authors have tackled the problem of the consultant's roles and style (Rutt, 1979; Brinko, 1990). The qualities recommended in a counselor may well serve as guidelines for the faculty developer who acts as messenger in the feedback process. For example, Kanfer and Goldstein (1986) see the key characteristics as credibility, empathy, warmth, self-disclosure, expertness, and status. While there may be some difference of opinion about the degree to which the messengers or consultants should be authoritative and linked to the reward system, there appears to be little doubt that they should be perceived as competent and expert in certain areas.

The Message

According to Bergquist and Phillips (1975), a message, once requested, should be descriptive, concrete, and presented in an atmosphere of trust. The first characteristic suggests an important contextual variable for feedback: information is appropriately presented only when the recipient has asked for it. In general, the whole evaluation process should be participative, and feedback should occur at a time when the recipient, by his or her own determination, is receptive. The more concrete, specific, and descriptive the feedback, the more easily one can respond to it. Kerr and Slocum (1981) and Murray (1987) suggest that feedback's content should be informative and provocative and contain information on consequences, as well as on behavior.

Form. The message can assume various forms. Direct records, such as videotapes of activities, have a strong impact on the viewer and contain a great deal of information. Preparation for discussion of the feedback should include an opportunity for the recipient to view the videotape record in private (partly for desensitization), as well as a rough guide on what to look for. A preview of the tape, followed by a discussion of major points on which to focus and then a second viewing, are recommended by some authors. Prose comments from students or peers are a more familiar kind of feedback and are reportedly preferred to statistical data (Ory and Braskamp, 1981; Tiberius, Sackin, and Cappe, 1987). Nevertheless, it is important to remember that because such comments often come from a small number of students, they should be interpreted with caution and only rarely, if ever, used in personnel decisions.

Kinds of Behavior. There are many sources of information about the kinds of items that can be used in a student rating questionnaire (see Chapter Six of this volume). The information may refer to very specific behaviors (supporting the recommendation that feedback be descriptive and concrete), or it may provide more global information. Cohen (1981) notes the distinction between information that leads to "within-class improvement" and information that addresses the more generic behaviors of instructional development, such as course design skills. If the purposes of the evaluation and feedback are clear, the kinds of behavior to be addressed should be obvious. For example, if the goal is immediate change in classroom performance, then information should be collected about specific classroom behaviors.

Timing. When should the message be presented? Psychological literature suggests immediate feedback, with a subsequent opportunity to rehearse an alternative performance. Tosti (1978) has suggested, in the context of performance appraisal, that positive feedback should immediately follow a session or activity, and that corrective feedback should be given immediately before the next occasion when the changes that it suggests can be implemented. Team teaching also provides an environment where continuous feedback can be presented soon after a session and close to the next one. At the very least, feedback should be presented when some action can be taken by the recipient. In this regard, the attraction of midterm feedback is obvious, but time should be scheduled for reactions and later action if the feedback is to have an impact.

Multiple Sources. A particular message gains credibility when it is one of a series of similar messages, from a variety of sources (see Chapter Five of this volume). People are used to asking for second opinions. Presentation of student examination scores could be accompanied by students' questionnaire data and a specialist's review of the course outline and teaching materials. Care should be taken, however, not to overwhelm the recipient with too much information (Russell, 1979). All available information need not be presented at one time. It is probably a good idea to encourage the recipient to request additional information.

Subsequent Messages. After a feedback session, additional information should be supplied. One obvious item is a written report on the session. Bergquist and Phillips (1975) suggest that it should be brief and fully documented, should protect the instructor's self-esteem, and should include arrangements for another diagnostic meeting.

The Recipient

One of the largest bodies of literature about human behavior addresses perception. The message that is sent is often not the message that is received. A teacher takes years to acquire a teaching repertoire and attitudes about teaching and learning. That acquired role is embedded in a particular personality, which affects perceptions related to the role. It is naive (and, in a sense, disrespectful) to assume that a few pieces of information about the teacher's "effectiveness" will change the recipient. Geis (1986) offers a detailed analysis of the many variables that affect the recipient when feedback is attempted. A few of these are discussed here.

Resistance and Denial. Resistance to information about ourselves is probably as common as self-reflection. If killing the messenger seems a bit too dramatic, denying the message is almost routine. The confrontation with others' perceptions of oneself, one's actions, and the consequences of those actions can be unnerving. "Clearly finding that one's favorite view of self is not similarly perceived by one's students makes one quite vulnerable" (Bess, 1979, p. 42).

Prerequisite Knowledge. Earlier, I mentioned the need for the recipient to be able to comprehend the information being relayed. "Information can be used for improvement and development only if the instructor knows how to interpret and apply the information" (Aleamoni and Stevens, 1983, p. 14). Information that is clear to the sender may be obscure to the recipient.

Past Experience and Individual Differences. Like any other group of human beings, postsecondary teachers have things in common, but they also differ on various dimensions. We can assume that resistance to or acceptance of feedback varies across teachers. Their positive or negative experiences with previous evaluations can influence their current attitudes. Ory, Brandenburg, and Pieper (1980) found that teachers who were regularly rated high tended to be more interested in collecting information about student achievement and less interested in learning about course management than were lower-rated instructors. Degree of familiarity with and skill in interpreting feedback data presumably have an effect on the nature and level of response, and so too might the degree to which a professor feels competent to change and take constructive action. Skill level of the professor can also direct the focus of feedback. McKeachie and others (1980) suggest that poorer teachers may require diagnosis and elimination of serious weaknesses, while better teachers may require clarification of their concepts of teaching, development of higher levels of skills, and enhancement of existing skills.

Self-Perception, Role Perception, and Discrepancy. Recipients have views of themselves and of their teaching role. A number of authors have illustrated how these perceptions and theories differ among professors (for example, Mann, Arnold, and Binder, 1970; Axelrod, 1973; Geis, 1982; Tiberius, 1986; Menges and Rando, 1989). Feedback may be given to a receiver who perceives the teaching role in a way quite different from the way or ways of the informants, and who may indeed have a view different from the one implied in the data-gathering instruments. If such a discrepancy does not lead to outright rejection of the feedback, it can make the feedback seem irrelevant or incomprehensible. For example, the teacher who sees the teaching-learning episode as a unique, idiosyncratic, spontaneous event will have difficulty in understanding low ratings from students on organization and planning.

It has been claimed that some discrepancy between a teacher's self-perception and feedback can be useful. Centra (1973) suggests that a moderate discrepancy between expected and obtained results on a questionnaire can serve to initiate action. Bergquist and Phillips (1975) agree that discrepancy is important for "unfreezing" the faculty client, as long as the discrepancy is not so great that it deflates the teacher's self-esteem. Discrepancies can be defined in different ways, and it is important to understand the subtleties of the evaluation data in presenting discrepancies to a client. For example, as Centra (1973) notes in a study that compared professors' self-ratings and ratings by students, although the ratings can be different between students and professors, a professor and students can still agree on the teacher's strong points and weaknesses.

Motivation and Skills. The perception of feedback, and the consequent action or nonaction, are partly functions of motivation and of skill and knowledge. It has often been said that there are only two kinds of performance problems: those in which the performer cannot take corrective action and those in which the performer can but will not. When one is aware that one cannot do something, it is not unusual to block out or deny information that bears on the absent skill. Our repertoires of skills and knowledge often affect our perceptions: "The instructor cannot effectively change unless the instructor knows how to change" (Aleamoni and Stevens, 1983, p. 14). To the extent that professors feel inadequate to change in the direction suggested by feedback or feel that the change would not involve their areas of greatest skill, they may be inclined to reject the information from the outset.

Motivation is a catchall word, devalued almost totally by its ambiguity in reference. Nevertheless, there certainly are many who can do things but will not do them (Davey and Sell, 1985). Again, perceptions of feedback may be critically influenced by general conditions such as a desire to improve, or by more specific conditions such as the aforementioned discrepancy. Many of the conditions that I have previously mentioned affect motivation. As Rotem and Glasman (1979, p. 504) note, "The university can do little to change its teachers' personalities, but it can do a lot about the context in which they operate." For example, if accepting and acting on feedback about instructional effectiveness is the norm of the group, the individual professor is likely to exhibit appropriate reactions.

The concept of locus of control is relevant to any discussion of motivation. The perceived degree of responsibility may affect interest in changing or improving performance. Thus, if I do not see the focal area of deficiency (say, for example, uninterested students) as one for which I am responsible, I may simply lack any interest in addressing it. Perceived ability to control or influence the situation is another contributor to motivational strength. If I see the admissions policy of the institution as the primary reason for poor quality students, then I may be disinclined to change my teaching practices when I am told of the high failure rate of students in my class: The critical variable is beyond my control.

The Immediate Environment

Obviously, discussions of feedback should be conducted in private and in an informal atmosphere. Another environmental feature is that the clients should perceive themselves as in control of the feedback sessions. This attribution of control may be made explicit in a number of ways, for instance, by allowing the client to determine the agenda of the meeting and reserving to the client the right to define the problem to be addressed (Davies, 1975). The literature shows agreement on the need for the environment to include a consultant, whether a peer, chairperson, or faculty developer (Aleamoni, 1978; Cohen, 1980; McKeachie and others, 1980; Aleamoni and Stevens, 1983; Menges and Brinko, 1986). "It is evident that when instructors are left to their own resources, ratings provide little help. Augmented feedback or, more specifically, expert consultation seems to be the key element for making student-rating data useable for improvement purposes" (Cohen, 1980, p. 338). As the tone of this chapter implies, I favor a collaborative rather than a prescriptive style for the consultant (Brinko, 1990 and Chapter Three of this volume).

Relevant to this discussion of the immediate environment is one important part of the consultant's job: offering structure for feedback meetings. "Feedback that is not accompanied by some focus has been found to change behavior little, if at all" (Fuller and Manning, 1973, p. 493). An agenda should be developed with the client and made explicit. Questions to be addressed include what the session is about, what the anticipated outcomes of the session are, what will be dealt with in the session, and, a more subtle point, what roles the participants will take. The elements of performance selected for possible change should be chosen with care. Performance elements that are satisfactory or better should be pointed out and emphasized. Among those elements that appear to need improvement, chosen targets should include behaviors that can be changed easily and will bring clear benefits to the teacher when changed (fewer student complaints, for example).

Consequences

The desired consequences or outcomes of the session are that the recipient has understood the feedback and has developed (or started to develop) some plans to deal with it. There should be a summing up of the feedback session, preferably, a report written by the consultant. Besides a description of the major observations and points made in the discussion, the report may include a plan or contract for future action and an agreement for further meetings. Feedback activities may have specific goals related to instructional improvement. If so, the behaviors to be changed should be those that will have an impact on something important to the client. A superordinate goal should be kept in mind: "That issue is how to enable persons to assume optimal responsibility for their learning while also ensuring that they receive adequate feedback about their performance" (Menges and others, 1988, p. 302). The good consultant, like the good teacher or parent, should encourage independence as a consequence of the feedback activities, and the client should become increasingly able to receive, interpret, and act on feedback. This approach is not merely a matter of philosophy: It has economic benefits for the faculty development system, for example, by turning more of the professional development activities over to the client. Resources must exist that enable the recipient to acquire knowledge and skills and try out new techniques, approaches, and models. One should expect feelings of discomfort and demonstrated awkwardness as outcomes of the feedback activities and related changes. When any behavioral change occurs, and when new skills and knowledge are being tried out, the new repertoires are likely to be dysfunctional. Time, guidance, and support are needed to develop them into smooth, integrated performances. This is a delicate time in the acquisition of new behavior. It is a time when the behavior can easily be inhibited by punishment. Assurance and encouragement are essential to move the performer beyond this tentative stage.

Summary

Administrators cannot simply continue to place personal blame for inadequate teaching on professors or to employ faculty developers to placate and goad professors into greater compliance with standards. The institution must recognize good teaching as a key goal and associate it with appropriate external rewards. Watts (1985, p. 1), having analyzed the reward system in a university division, concluded "that the university needed to be more holistic in its approach to organizational control and more knowledgeable about the faculty and work situation. A contingency approach to the system was recommended." Watts avoids simplistic recommendations, noting, for example, the importance of intrinsic as well as external rewards, stressing the need for (but the dangers inherent to) the establishment of performance standards, and recognizing the importance of matching the individual to the teaching task. Watts's conclusion can also be applied to teaching improvement and, in particular, to the feedback process. The effective consultant is aware of context, sender, message, recipient, environment, and consequences, and of their relationship to and possible effects on the feedback process.

This chapter has presented a number of issues and concepts related to positive and effective feedback interactions. In order to provide a succinct and useful reference, these considerations have been outlined in Exhibit 1.1. It is my hope that this outline will help teaching consultants prepare for the "moment of truth" when they provide feedback to their faculty clients.

Exhibit 1.1. Putting It All Together

The Context

1. Feedback should be part of a comprehensive plan for evaluation and development.
2. The plan should be developed with the participation of the person who receives the feedback.
3. The purposes and goals of the plan and of the feedback sessions should be explicit and specific.
4. Information should be derived from several different sources.
5. The information-gathering techniques—indeed, the whole evaluation plan—should have demonstrable technical validity.
6. The effort should be fair, as well as sound.
7. The atmosphere in which the evaluation is carried out should be positive, supportive, and cooperative. The evaluation should be a serious activity, that is, serve a continuous function in the organization as part of its program for personal and professional development.

The Sender and the Message

1. The sender should be credible, trustworthy, and empathetic and should be seen as having expertise. He or she should not be identified with career decision-making authorities, for a sender cannot function well if perceived as a spy and a judge as well as a facilitator.
2. The feedback message should be couched in terms that are clear to the recipient. It should be credible, descriptive, and concrete. It should address concerns of interest to the recipient and be delivered at a time when the recipient wishes to receive the information. It may well include such points of reference as group norms for statistical data. It should be delivered soon after the performance to which it refers, and time should be made available for discussion and for experimentation with and acquisition of new behavior.

The Recipient and the Immediate Environment

1. The recipient should have a sense of control over the feedback process (for example, setting the agenda and establishing the focus of the feedback session).
2. The recipient should be prepared for feedback. For example, self-instructional materials can assist the recipient in understanding statistical information. The opportunity to preview videotapes made in the recipient's classroom can desensitize the recipient and help him or her develop foci for later discussion.
3. The feedback process should include consultation with a person trained in interpreting feedback information and providing counseling. This consultant should be knowledgeable about resources for personal and professional development (for useful guidelines on providing a teaching critique, see Carroll and Goldberg, 1989).

The Consequences

1. The environment should be conducive to the suggested changes. In short, improvements in teaching should be rewarded by the system.

Exhibit 1.1. *(continued)*

2. Resources should exist to help recipients make changes suggested by feedback data. "The usefulness of student rating feedback is ensured only when [it is] integrated with a system of instructional support. . . . A critical aspect of the instructional support system involves training the instructor in how to effect instructional improvement" (Aleamoni and Stevens, 1983, p. 3).
3. Feedback activity should lead to the cooperative development of an improvement plan that, when implemented, produces more feedback for further adjustment and improvement.

References

Aleamoni, L. M. "The Usefulness of Student Evaluations in Improving College Teaching." *Instructional Science,* 1978, 7 (1), 95–105.

Aleamoni, L. M., and Stevens, J. J. "The Effectiveness of Consultation in Support of Student Evaluation Feedback: A Ten-Year Follow-up." Paper presented at the annual meetings of the Rocky Mountain Psychological Association, Albuquerque, New Mexico, April–May 1983.

Axelrod, J. *The University Teacher as Artist.* San Francisco: Jossey-Bass, 1973.

Bergquist, W. H., and Phillips, S. R. "Components of an Effective Faculty Development Program." *Journal of Higher Education,* 1975, 46 (2), 177–211.

Bess, J. L. "The Social Psychology of Commitment to College Teaching." Paper presented at the 63rd annual meetings of the American Association for Higher Education, Washington, D.C., March 1979.

Brinko, K. T. "Instructional Consultation with Feedback in Higher Education." *Journal of Higher Education,* 1990, 61 (1), 65–83.

Cannon, W. B. *The Wisdom of the Body.* New York: Norton, 1932.

Carroll, J. G., and Goldberg, S. R. "Teaching Consultants: A Collegial Approach to Better Teaching." *College Teaching,* 1989, 37 (4), 143–146.

Centra, J. A. "Self-Ratings of College Teachers: A Comparison with Student Ratings." *Journal of Educational Measurement,* 1973, 10 (4), 287–295.

Centra, J. A. "Formative and Summative Evaluation: Parody or Paradox?" In L. M. Aleamoni (ed.), *Techniques for Evaluating and Improving Instruction.* New Directions for Teaching and Learning, no. 31. San Francisco: Jossey-Bass, 1987.

Clark, J., and Beckey, J. "Use of Small Groups in Instructional Evaluation." *POD Quarterly,* 1979, 1, 87–95.

Cohen, P. A. "Effectiveness of Student-Rating Feedback for Improving College Instruction: A Meta-Analysis of Findings." *Research in Higher Education,* 1980, 13 (4), 321–341.

Cohen, P. A. "Using Student Ratings to Improve Instruction: A Synthesis of Findings." Paper presented at the 65th annual meetings of the American Educational Research Association, Los Angeles, April 1981.

Davey, K. B., and Sell, G. R. "Instructional Evaluation for Development/Improvement: Fact or Fiction?" Paper presented at the 69th annual meetings of the American Educational Research Association, Chicago, March–April 1985.

Davies, I. K. "Some Aspects of a Theory of Advice: The Management of an Instructional Developer-Client, Evaluator-Client Relationship." *Instructional Science,* 1975, 3 (4), 351–373.

Fuhrman, B. S., and Grasha, A. F. *A Practical Handbook for College Teachers.* Boston: Little, Brown, 1983.

Fuller, F. F., and Manning, B. A. "Self-Confrontation Reviewed: A Conceptualization for Video Playback in Teacher Education." *Review of Educational Research,* 1973, *43* (4), 469–528.

Geis, G. L. "Perceptions of Teaching and How They Affect Teaching Improvement Efforts." In *Improving University Teaching: Proceedings of the Seventh International Conference.* College Park: University of Maryland and University College/University of Tsukuba, 1982.

Geis, G. L. "Formative Evaluation: The Receiving Side." *Performance and Instruction,* 1986, *25* (5), 1–8.

Gil, D. H. "Instructional Evaluation as a Feedback Process." In L. M. Aleamoni (ed.), *Techniques for Evaluating and Improving Instruction.* New Directions for Teaching and Learning, no. 31. San Francisco: Jossey-Bass, 1987.

Kanfer, F. H., and Goldstein, A. P. *Helping People Change: A Textbook of Methods.* (3rd ed.) Elmsford, N.Y.: Pergamon, 1986.

Kerr, S., and Slocum, J. W. "Controlling the Performance of People in Organizations." In P. C. Nystrom and W. H. Starbuck (eds.), *Handbook of Organizational Design.* Vol. 2: *Remodeling Organizations and Their Environments.* New York: Oxford University Press, 1981.

McKeachie, W. J., Lin, Y-G., Daugherty, M., Moffett, M. M., Neigler, C., Nork, J., Walz, M., and Baldwin, R. "Using Student Ratings and Consultation to Improve Instruction." *British Journal of Educational Psychology,* 1980, *50* (2), 168–174.

Mann, R. D., Arnold, S., and Binder, J. *The College Classroom: Conflict, Change, and Learning.* New York: Wiley, 1970.

Menges, R. J., and Brinko, K. T. "Effects of Student Evaluation Feedback: A Meta-Analysis of Higher Education Research." Paper presented at the 70th annual meetings of the American Educational Research Association, San Francisco, April 1986. (ED 270 408)

Menges, R. J., Mathis, B. C., Halliburton, D., Marincovich, M., and Svinicki, M. "Strengthening Professional Development: Lessons from the Program for Faculty Renewal at Stanford." *Journal of Higher Education,* 1988, *59* (3), 291–304.

Menges, R. J., and Rando, W. C. "What Are Your Assumptions? Improving Instruction by Examining Theories." *College Teaching,* 1989, *37* (2), 54–60.

Murray, H. G. "Acquiring Student Feedback That Improves Instruction." In M. G. Weimer (ed.), *Teaching Large Classes Well.* New Directions for Teaching and Learning, no. 32. San Francisco: Jossey-Bass, 1987.

Ory, J. C., Brandenburg, D. C., and Pieper, D. M. "Selection of Course Evaluation Items by High- and Low-Rated Faculty of Varying Academic Ranks." *Research in Higher Education,* 1980, *12* (3), 245–253.

Ory, J. C., and Braskamp, L. A. "Faculty Perceptions of the Quality and Usefulness of Three Types of Evaluative Information." *Research in Higher Education,* 1981, *15* (3), 271–282.

Rotem, A., and Glasman, N. S. "On the Effectiveness of Students' Evaluative Feedback to University Professors." *Review of Educational Research,* 1979, *49* (3), 497–511.

Russell, T. L. "What Does Practice Teaching Teach?" *Education Canada,* 1979, *19* (1), 6–11, 15.

Rutt, D. P. "An Investigation of the Consultation Styles of Instructional Developers." Unpublished doctoral dissertation, Instructional Systems Technology, Indiana University, 1979.

Seldin, P., and Associates. *How Administrators Can Improve Teaching: Moving from Talk to Action in Higher Education.* San Francisco: Jossey-Bass, 1990.

Tiberius, R. G. "Metaphors Underlying the Improvement of Teaching and Learning." *British Journal of Educational Technology*, 1986, *17* (2), 144-156.

Tiberius, R. G., Sackin, H. D., and Cappe, L. "A Comparison of Two Methods for Evaluating Teaching." *Studies in Higher Education*, 1987, *12* (3), 287-297.

Tosti, D. T. "Formative Feedback." *National Society for Performance and Instruction Journal*, 1978, *17* (8), 19-21.

Tuckman, B. W., and Oliver, W. F. "Effectiveness of Feedback to Teachers as a Function of Source." *Journal of Educational Psychology*, 1968, *59* (4), 297-301.

Watts, L. "Assessment of Organizational and Control Systems." Unpublished manuscript, Arizona State University, 1985.

Wiener, N. *Cybernetics: Control and Communication in the Animal and the Machine.* Cambridge, Mass.: MIT Press, 1948.

George L. Geis is professor in the Higher Education Group at the Ontario Institute for Studies in Education, Toronto, Ontario, Canada.

The only realistic approach to faculty development is one that views teaching from a faculty perspective.

The Real World of Teaching Improvement: A Faculty Perspective

Robert J. Menges

> The pressure of my department for good evaluations has put enough pressure on me that I often find myself thinking of my students as the enemy and these forms as the weapons they use in a thoughtless way to damage me. The last time I handed them out I nearly got sick to my stomach before class [anonymous teaching assistant, quoted in Hoffmann and Oseroff-Varnell, 1989, p. 6].

> I must say that I have learned little from these evaluations. It is good to know that one's teaching is appreciated, of course, but even the most gushing student praise does not allay self-doubts about not being as good at the job as one ought to be. In fact, in my own case, the only aid I have received from student evaluations is the single-sentence comment "He jiggles the change in his pockets." As a result of this penetrating criticism, I now put all my change in my briefcase before stepping into a classroom [Epstein, 1981, p. xiii].

> It would seem reasonable enough that those who make their living by teaching might be responsive to being taught. Alas, I fear it is not so. Most people resist being taught what they already think they know. Professors resist strongly, and usually in proportion to the felt pressure being applied from the outside [Eble, 1983, p. 134].

While it is true that only teachers can improve their teaching, it is also true that improvements are greater when teachers do not have to make them entirely on their own. Improvement depends not only on teachers' impulses toward excellence but also on external assistance. Faculty development programs can assist by helping teachers cope with the apprehension that evaluation naturally triggers, by pointing out what evaluative information is most worthwhile to solicit from students, by advising about other sources of helpful information, and by demonstrating alternative approaches to teaching and learning, but not much will happen if those efforts fail to engage the real world of academic life as faculty experience it.

In this chapter, I attempt to write about that world from the faculty's perspective. In the first sections, I describe faculty's views of the academic profession and, more narrowly, of teaching. I then argue that professors' inclinations to seek information about the results of their work—their natural feedback-seeking behavior—can serve as a practical and effective focus for evaluation and development programs.

Faculty's Views of the Profession: Optimism and Stress

There is much to admire and even to envy in the work of the college professor. By comparison with many other jobs, hours are flexible, pay is good, activities are varied, and co-workers are bright and stimulating. Further, there are opportunities to affect the future. Academics can significantly influence knowledge and public policy through their scholarly and creative work and, indirectly, through students.

Surveys confirm a largely positive outlook among professors. In a 1989 Carnegie Foundation survey (Mooney, 1989) of 5,450 professors, more than 9 out of 10 agreed that their institutions were either very good (49 percent) or fairly good (43 percent) places to work. By contrast with Carnegie surveys in 1969, 1975, and 1984, faculty views have become increasingly optimistic (selected survey results are shown in Table 2.1). Although the respondents appear generally optimistic (item 1), there are indications of problems. Preparation of undergraduates is seen as inadequate: 3 out of 4 respondents agree that students are underprepared in basic skills (item 2). The sense of community in institutions is also problematic: Only 37 percent agree that it is good or excellent (item 3). Evaluation procedures are troublesome: 2 out of 3 respondents agree that better ways are needed to evaluate scholarly performance (item 4). Overall, 44 percent agree strongly or with reservations with the statement "My job is the source of considerable personal strain" (item 5), and the rate of agreement is considerably higher among women than among men.

The nature of problems sensed by faculty is clarified by responses to other survey items. Even though faculty find students underprepared, 7 out of 10 say that enhancement of creative thinking is a very important goal of undergraduate education (item 6). Since enhancement of creative thinking is a formidable challenge, even when students are well prepared, attempts

Table 2.1. Percentage of Faculty Agreeing with Selected Items from Carnegie Foundation Survey

Survey Items	All	ResUniv	LibArts	Men	Women
1. In general, my institution is a "very good" or "fairly good" place for me.	92	90	92	93	92
2. The undergraduates with whom I have close contact are seriously underprepared in basic skills such as those required for written and oral communication.	75	68	64	74	77
3. The sense of community at this institution is "excellent" or "good."	37	25	56	35	38
4. At my institution, we need better ways, besides publications, to evaluate the scholarly performance of faculty.	68	69	69	68	68
5. My job is the source of considerable personal strain.	44	48	48	40	51
6. Enhancing creative thinking is a very important goal of the undergraduate curriculum.	70	72	79	69	73
7. I enjoy interacting informally with undergraduates outside the classroom.	83	77	92	84	81
8. My major interest is in teaching or is leaning toward teaching.	71	35	84	67	78
9. Teaching effectiveness should be the primary criterion for promotion of faculty.	62	22	76	58	73
10. In my department it is difficult for a person to achieve tenure if he or she does not publish.	54	94	39	57	45
11. The pressure to publish reduces the quality of teaching at my institution.	35	52	22	36	34
12. Relationships with undergraduates are an aspect of higher education considered very important.	57	36	72	54	62

Source: Adapted from Mooney, 1989.

to reach this goal with poorly prepared students are bound to lead to frustration. Despite faculty's dissatisfaction with the sense of community on campus, 8 out of 10 agree that they enjoy interacting informally with undergraduates outside the classroom (item 7). Thus, it appears that faculty are seeking community in an environment where community is not very likely, and this issue is exacerbated at research universities. Finally, while faculty's interests are in teaching or lean toward teaching (71 percent), and while 6 of 10 faculty members agree that teaching effectiveness should be the primary criterion for promotion (items 8 and 9), the pressure to publish is seen by about one-third as detrimental to the quality of teaching, especially in research universities (items 10 and 11). Differences between men and women further complicate this issue.

A nationwide survey of academics conducted in 1982 identified more precisely what faculty feel is stressful (Gmelch, Lovrich, and Wilke, 1984). Among major sources of work-related stress was ambiguity in the criteria used to evaluate faculty's teaching, research, and service, and this ambiguity was greatest for teaching. Some of the stressors identified in that survey are external and are related to institutional constraints, such as salary levels and financial support for research, but one stressor is internal: More than half the respondents indicated that "setting excessively high self-expectations" is a serious source of work-related stress. Overall, that is the highest-rated source of stress in the survey.

Faculty who set excessively high expectations for themselves are likely to be unrealistic about job requirements. In academia, several attributes of work militate against realistic expectations. First, college faculty are hired on the basis of educational and scholarly attainments. They devote most of their time to teaching, advising, and service. They advance (at least partly) on the basis of scholarly and creative accomplishments. Since none of these activities meshes fully with the others, conflict is built into the job. Second, most faculty have had little or no systematic training for teaching, and there are few resources and incentives to perfect instructional skills on the job. Third, teaching occurs in isolation from colleagues, and faculty lack systematic opportunities to observe and discuss the instructional enterprise. Fourth, teaching effectiveness is hard to gauge, since educational outcomes are rarely stated specifically enough or evaluated soon enough to permit useful feedback about changes in students. Fifth, work patterns for teaching and scholarship are often in conflict. Teaching is subject to rhythms of the academic calendar, whereas scholarly rhythms, for the most part, are internal. Because they need not coincide with institutional schedules and thus may seem less urgent, these creative rhythms may well be neglected. Neglect of these rhythms is especially likely during the early stages of a career, precisely when the cost of neglect is greatest.

These characteristics of academic work raise serious issues for teaching improvement. Ideally, professionals work in an environment rich in information and communication about objectives, where expectations are clear and where rewards are contingent on demonstrated effective performance. The real world of college teaching, however, is quite different. It tends to be poor in information about objectives and outcomes, largely isolated, always hurried, subject to evaluations based on ambiguous criteria, and dependent on performance criteria from domains other than teaching. I believe that this situation can be changed most easily and dramatically by increasing the amount of available information about the effects of teaching and by stimulating communication among faculty about teaching. As we go about making those changes, we must take into account the beliefs and assumptions that faculty hold about teaching and learning.

Faculty's Views of Teaching: Beliefs and Practices

Faculty differ in their views of teaching and learning, both by disposition and by circumstances of employment. For some, teaching is a calling, an all-consuming vocation. For others, instructional responsibilities merely consume time better devoted to other professional responsibilities. Most of us seek a workable compromise to reconcile these extremes.

Research shows that professors vary in their informal or implicit theories about teaching. Since most academics have little training in the field of education, it is not surprising that their theories about teaching and learning are less sophisticated than their theories about research specialties. Many college teachers, especially those with little experience, describe students as if they were containers to be filled or objects to be shaped or molded. Teachers with more experience are likely to hold somewhat more complex views, in which learners are seen as active participants in teaching and learning (Fox, 1983).

When my colleagues and I asked graduate teaching assistants (TAs) what they meant by the term *teaching,* we found three kinds of responses. About one-third were oriented toward content ("My giving them knowledge and them really understanding it"). Another third were oriented toward process ("Give them the means to go on and look at questions and answer the questions themselves"). The rest were motivation- or affect-oriented ("The number one priority seems to be students' interest in the subject"). Implicit theories are related to what teachers do in problem situations (or at least to what they say they do). When TAs discussed how they would react in a class where students were reluctant to participate in discussion, a clear pattern emerged. Most TAs who were content- or motivation-oriented indicated that they would default in the face of silent students, perhaps by dismissing the class. TAs oriented toward process, by contrast, were likely to say that they would persist by rephrasing questions or trying to stimulate discussion in some other way (Menges and Rando, 1989).

Another important difference among college teachers concerns achievement style. In a study of university faculty, Braskamp, Fowler, and Ory (1984) found two achievement styles. Faculty with the *direct* style primarily use their own efforts to attain achievement, whereas those with the *relational* style achieve for and through their relationships with others. Of fifteen assistant professors interviewed, thirteen were direct achievers. The two who were relational had a primary interest in helping students develop and achieve. The pattern is somewhat different at higher faculty ranks. Seven of fifteen associate professors were at least partly relational achievers, and eleven of eighteen full professors had an achievement style that combined the direct and the relational. There appears to be some conflict between achievement style and source of work satisfaction. At all ranks, despite a direct achievement style, most faculty reported that teaching and interacting with students were their major sources of satisfaction.

Faculty at liberal arts colleges and two-year colleges appear to hold quite different views. In the Carnegie survey, for example (see Table 2.1), about 70 percent of respondents from these colleges consider relationships with undergraduates very important as compared with only about one-third from research universities (item 12). In studies of faculty motivation, Maehr and Braskamp (1986) found that a striving for excellence was more characteristic of university professors and that social concern for others was more characteristic of professors at small colleges.

Even faculty who are strongly oriented toward students and toward teaching vary in their beliefs about educational goals (as any meeting of a curriculum committee reveals). Failure to make beliefs explicit often leads to dissension, since these beliefs act as filters through which faculty interpret information about students, about what is taught, and about how teaching should be conducted. Disagreements about course content, about teaching effectiveness, and about criteria for successful learning may well be traced to differences in unarticulated beliefs and assumptions.

Research into how faculty plan introductory courses has revealed that the discipline is a fundamental influence (Stark, Lowther, Bentley, and Martens, 1990). One's disciplinary home has a far stronger effect on course planning than does the context or situation in which one teaches. Implicit assumptions about students and about learning must be made explicit if there is to be fruitful cross-disciplinary dialogue.

Not all faculty are willing to reflect on their beliefs and practices. Some cling to a holistic, vaguely romantic notion, as if teaching were too delicate to withstand examination: Because teaching is ephemeral, it eludes analysis. Like love, teaching can be experienced, contemplated, and celebrated, but it can never be understood. At the other extreme are technologists who relish analyzing and even dismembering teaching into components, factors, and flowcharts. They regard teaching as little more than a process of specifying objectives, developing teaching activities consistent with those objectives, engaging learners in the activities, assessing outcomes, and planning revisions for the next teaching occasion. The views of most college teachers, somewhere between these extremes, imply that while teaching can withstand examination, it is never fully understood through reductive analysis. Change and improvement are possible, but shortages of time and resources limit their impact. Teachers develop instructional routines that include teaching, reflection on information about successes and failures, and then teaching again, with attempts to make changes based on feedback. This scheme (teaching-feedback-teaching) assumes a search for equilibrium, in which a disturbance leads to adjustments and equilibrium returns after adjustments are made. The following section provides more detail about the nature of these disturbances and adjustments.

Seeking and Using Feedback

With all the work that professors must do, teaching is not always meticulously planned and brilliantly executed. The teach-feedback-teach scheme acknowledges this reality, and its emphasis on feedback permits refinement and revision, both while instruction is in progress and as a result of more leisurely deliberation and planning.

To illustrate a feedback loop, consider the familiar example of a household thermostat. A decrease in room temperature is sensed by the thermometer (input). The thermostat (comparator) checks temperature data against its setting (standard) and switches the furnace on. Heat from the furnace (output) raises room temperature and returns the system to equilibrium (see Figure 2.1). Feedback loops are easily discerned in instructional settings. Imagine that examination scores create dissonance because the teacher (comparator) finds them below her standard. She may deal with the discrepancy by gathering additional kinds of data, ultimately concluding that students are not deficient after all. Thus, equilibrium is restored. She may reflect on what she expects of students, decide that these expectations are too high, and adjust her expectations to restore equilibrium. Finally, she may schedule review sessions, in order to raise students' performance, thereby restoring equilibrium.

Examination of the feedback loop helps us differentiate and name these three ways of restoring equilibrium. To adjust the nature and timing of available information is to restore equilibrium through input. To adjust expectations, beliefs, and values is to restore equilibrium through standards. To adjust instructional behaviors and methods is to restore equilibrium through output. In each case, the goal is to correct a disturbance and restore the system to a steady state (Menges, 1987).

Many college teachers do this naturally. They solicit information as feedback; they reflect on their expectations, beliefs, and values; and they experiment with different ways of teaching. Sometimes, however, the information that they obtain is incomplete and biased; sometimes it is interpreted hastily or used inconsistently.

Figure 2.1. A Simple Feedback Loop

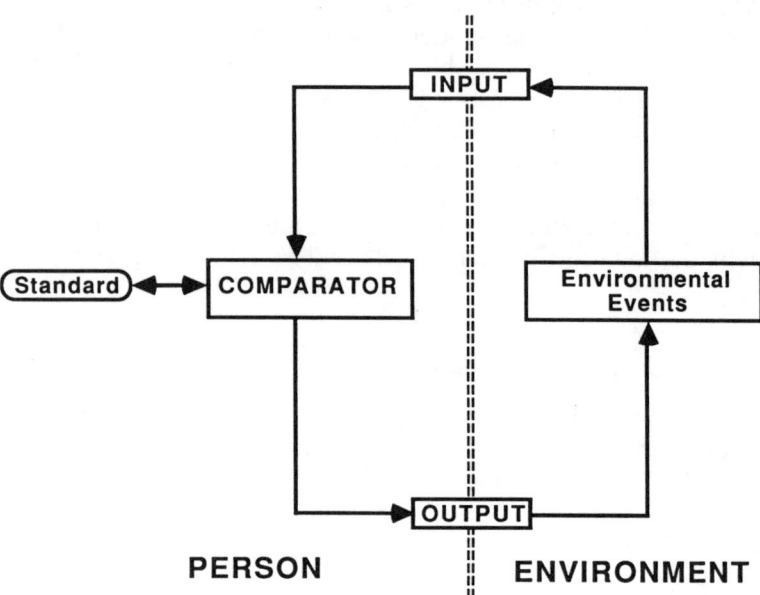

Improving Information. To improve information fed back to teachers is to alter input. Geis's feedback model (see Chapter One) includes the sender, the message, the recipient, and the consequences. Exhibit 2.1 lists a number of sources of information like those discussed by Geis. From the faculty's perspective, important distinctions must be made among the items on this list.

Teacher perceptions during class are no doubt the most frequently used feedback. TAs tell us repeatedly that they scan students' faces during class to determine how things are going: "I would say that the blank look, the blank stare, is a pretty good gauge, an indication that the class has not been successful. Now, if students are nodding vigorously or shaking their heads furiously, either of those reactions, I don't mind at all, because it means they will go and think about the issues raised in class." TAs also attend to behavioral cues as the class ends: "The most important criterion is the enthusiasm that the students leave with, because a really successful class is the kind where I have to stop them from talking five minutes after the section is over, because I've got to go to my next section" (Shaeffer, McGill, and Menges, 1989, p. 177). Because perceptions during class are immediate and concrete, they have great impact. They may even be regarded as sufficient for indicating one's effectiveness. As a professor

Exhibit 2.1. Feedback Sources

Classroom Information
   Teacher perceptions during class
   Audio- and videotapes

Student Opinion
   Student surveys (closed questions)
   Student surveys (open questions)
   Student informal comments
   Student interviews (individual)
   Student interviews (group)

Alumni Opinion
   Alumni informal comments
   Alumni surveys

Student Learning
   Student course examinations
   Student papers and other graded work
   Student standardized test scores

Collegial Information
   Supervisor visit
   Teaching consultant visit
   Colleague visit
   Colleague assessment of teaching materials
   Colleague informal comments

said, "If I come out of class feeling good, that's how I rate my performance" (Braskamp, Fowler, and Ory, 1981, p. 4).

When feedback is limited to real-time perceptions of classroom events, the teacher risks considerable error. In a busy classroom, the teacher is hardly an objective or comprehensive observer. New teachers especially feel overloaded and have nowhere to store everything that they perceive. Experienced teachers may find it easier to deal with large amounts of classroom information. They have developed what Peterson and Comeaux (1987) call "mental scaffolding," which helps them understand classroom events. Because of these structures, they are able to retain and retrieve more information and to analyze it in more sophisticated ways than are novice teachers. Storage of classroom events on audiotape or videotape makes information somewhat easier to manage, but time is required for reviewing the tape and reducing the information to usable form. It may also be necessary to have someone else interpret the information and discuss the implications for teaching.

Information fed back by students takes a number of forms. End-of-course questionnaires are widely institutionalized, and Murray (1987) summarizes surveys showing faculty's acceptance of and satisfaction with such information as a useful aid to teaching. It is clear from research that student rating feedback can be effective, particularly when consultation is provided (Menges and Brinko, 1986).

From the faculty's perspective, student rating feedback raises three major problems for the task of improving teaching. One problem involves difficulties in understanding the feedback and what it implies for teaching (Franklin and Theall, 1989). The second problem is the impersonality of an institutionalized system. Many of the students' evaluations are discarded without having been read because the teacher has no investment in the questions that they contain and little trust in the procedures by which information was gathered. The third problem is the apprehension that naturally accompanies evaluative information. Faculty interviewed by Braskamp, Fowler, and Ory (1981) were quite open about their anxiety over receiving evaluative information. Less experienced teachers, like the TA quoted at the beginning of this chapter, are likely to be even more apprehensive. One defense is to keep some psychological distance from the data: "In general, many of the things I do are not solely an attempt to get higher ratings. Most I do just because I believe they're effective" (Hoffmann and Oseroff-Varnell, 1989, p. 5). As professionals, most teachers voluntarily solicit feedback; as vulnerable human beings, it is quite natural to feel threatened by unsolicited and possibly irrelevant feedback.

Some of these problems are reduced when faculty's participation and control are increased. Faculty may choose some of the questionnaire items. Open-ended questions may be included, students' comments may be gathered through interviews, and reports may take narrative rather than statistical forms. The resulting information is likely to be more credible to faculty (Ory and Braskamp, 1981), but its value will be limited in other ways. For example, questionnaire items drafted by faculty may be poorly worded unless chosen from pretested, validated lists, and students selected for interviews may be unrepresentative unless a sampling plan has been carefully prepared. As seen in Exhibit 2.1, former students and alumni can also feed back potentially valuable information, although this feedback is subject to the same limitations as information from current students.

Some argue that changes in students constitute the information of greatest relevance for teaching improvement. Examinations, papers, lab reports, and other graded work are undoubtedly informative, as is information about students' study habits and their scores on standardized tests. The major problems with using information about learning to improve teaching are that graded work is an incomplete representation of intended learning outcomes, it is difficult to connect particular features of teaching with specific learning outcomes, and some important influences on learning are beyond the teacher's control.

The last five items listed in Exhibit 2.1 are feedback sources that involve expertise different from that of students. Supervisors provide administrative expertise, teaching consultants provide pedagogical expertise, and colleagues provide discipline-related expertise. Advice from any of these sources is potentially threatening and is probably best received when the teacher both voluntarily requests it and confers with the expert prior to a classroom visit.

Reviewing Standards. Feedback models strike some as excessively mechanistic and reductionistic, unable to reflect the complexities of teaching and learning. I disagree, primarily because standards reflect the intentionality of human behavior. There is no intentionality in mechanical systems. Standards for mechanical systems are set from outside (for example, the homeowner sets the thermostat). In human situations, standards can be set from within the system—when, for example, the teacher adjusts his or her expectations while carrying on a kind of conversation between personal values and external constraints: "What the machines leave out is a discussion of the values underlying the messages, and the creative generation of new ideas. What we do not see is the furnace answering the thermostat in this way: 'Yes, I know; it's cold again. But I'm working very inefficiently at this level of output. Couldn't we reconsider the temperature setting? A few degrees colder is probably healthier for our bosses anyway. Besides, it will give them a chance to wear those new sweaters they bought last weekend. I think that we should get together with them and thrash this thing out' " (Tiberius, 1986, p. 154). This kind of conversation, foreign to machines, is natural to humans.

The impulse to review standards springs from external as well as internal sources. The kinds of information (input) discussed in the preceding section illustrate external sources, and that input is surely sufficient to occasion examination and reexamination of standards. Review of standards may also be stimulated from within by the teacher's curiosity or predispositions. Stevens (1988, p. 67) quotes a professor of communications who continually tinkers with her teaching: "I seek teaching as a creative act. I love thinking up new ways to do things or designing activities or problem solving and it's almost an aesthetic performance. . . . It's like when I design a way to get something across, I take pleasure in the thing itself. . . . It's not just that it works but I get a real intellectual pleasure out of the puzzle part of it." This teacher seems driven both by intellectual curiosity and by an aesthetic sensibility.

Some teachers are particularly sensitive to cues from others about how they are perceived. These so-called self-monitors scan the environment for such cues and make adjustments accordingly (Snyder, 1979). In other words, they are predisposed to seek feedback and to assess it in relation to their own standards.

Standards are also clarified in confrontation with alternative models of teaching. Models such as teacher as expert, teacher as manager, and teacher as facilitator are excellent stimuli for discussion. When discussing these models with colleagues or viewing videotapes of teachers who exemplify contrasting styles, faculty cannot escape reflection on their own values about teaching.

Questionnaires about teachers' and students' goals are another tool for examining values. The Teaching Goals Inventory, a product of the Classroom Research Project (Cross and Angelo, 1989), asks faculty to indicate the importance of a large number of possible course goals: mastering knowledge of subject matter, developing creative openness to new ideas, preparing for more advanced education, collaborating and working productively with others, synthesizing and integrating information and ideas from different sources, and so on. When responses are compared across departments or across campuses, it is enlightening to learn how one's own preferences compare with the preferences of those who teach courses intended to have similar goals.

With respect to standards, some limitations of the single feedback loop become clear. Most instructional situations have multiple feedback loops that are hierarchically arranged. Because a particular course is affected by much more than its immediate circumstances, standards can be reviewed in relation to feedback loops at other levels, including loops within the institution and loops that connect the institution with its external constituencies. For example, a teacher may raise standards for students' performance as part of an effort to increase the institution's selectivity. This adjustment of standards leads to dissonance, since the task of weeding out poor students causes considerable disruption. The system is ultimately likely to regain equilibrium, but at a different level than before. Disruption is not necessarily undesirable, but it is important that the imbalance be brief, since systems out of balance are unstable and risk self-destruction. Out-of-balance systems survive "when the imbalance is of short duration and when it is part of a superordinate feedback loop in a higher-level system" (Menges, 1987, p. 5).

Enhancing Teaching Repertoires. To increase the variety and quality of instructional skills is to alter output. This output is based on intentions about new and future behaviors that are derived by comparing input with standards, but intentions will surely go awry if instructors lack the skills necessary for implementing them.

What skills are needed depends on many circumstances, although the ways to improve teaching are not very numerous. In a book about instructional consultation, Povlacs (1988, p. 240) observes, "Most recommendations for improving teaching can be grouped into relatively few categories: organizing materials meaningfully and clearly, relating to students, improving classroom communication, designing equitable methods of testing and grading, and increasing active learning. The faculty member as the subject matter expert must ultimately make the precise application to the material."

A psychology teacher who was participating in Stevens's (1988, p. 69) study described a problem with the students in a large class who were doing field projects: "I couldn't possibly see them all tutorially. So I thought of putting them into small groups and asking them to explicitly talk to each other about their projects, to give explicit suggestions for other activities, recording techniques, or anything else." Pleased with that change, the teacher went farther when the course was next offered by giving an agenda to each group that would help guide discussion. The agenda dealt with substantive ideas as well as group members' communication patterns. Still hoping for more student contact, she decided to meet with each group in her office. In subsequent terms, further refinements were introduced. None of these changes required her to learn new or difficult skills.

Other teachers in that study engaged in a similar "pattern of continual adjustment." As Stevens says, they "tinkered" with their teaching. They tried a small variation in instructional approach, attended to its effects, and further modified subsequent teaching. A professor of communications described the process in this way: "It's not like a pendulum, switching back and forth between techniques. It's more like a bedspring. Instead of swinging back and forth, you kind of circle around. You pick up something you were doing before, but this time when you use it, you use it differently" (Stevens, 1988, p. 69).

In the real world of college teaching, I suspect that more faculty change through such tinkering than they do as a result of workshops and other formal programs. This does not mean that teaching-improvement programs are superfluous or unjustifiable, but it leaves us with questions about what goals are appropriate for improvement programs and about the form that these programs should take.

Faculty-Centered Evaluation and Development

I have been considering only the teaching domain, leaving aside all the nonteaching activities of faculty, and I have been concerned with evaluation for improvement, rather than with evaluation primarily for personnel review. Thus, I omit much that faculty do and much that is evaluated. It is clear that even the limited portion of the world of faculty discussed here is crowded and hurried. Nevertheless, most faculty manage their work competently and relish their autonomy as they design courses, plan instructional activities, experiment, and innovate. Unfortunately, most approaches to faculty development limit these admirably self-reliant people by putting them into relatively passive roles.

In four of the five most common approaches to faculty development (Angelo, 1989), faculty are made the objects of activities largely initiated and conducted by others: lectures and demonstrations, awards ceremonies, workshops and seminars, consultations, and observation and structured conversation. In all categories but the last, faculty are likely to be spectators, recipients, trainees, clients; only in the last approach do faculty participate as partners, exercising significant authority in shaping their experiences. Thus, faculty development opportunities may actually inhibit rather than support autonomy and initiative. When faculty development agencies impose agendas on faculty, the consequences are negative. Attendance and participation decline, and faculty may settle into the role of passive students or even resentful conscripts.

If we attempt to center on faculty, rather than on programs and services, what will faculty development activities look like? Here are a few suggestions keyed to components of the feedback model. These activities are not new or unique, but here they are described in ways that keep faculty at the center.

Faculty-Centered Feedback. When teaching improvement is the goal, we should provide resources that facilitate natural feedback seeking, rather than institutionalize feedback systems that provide standardized information to faculty about their performance. This perspective makes feedback a personal resource rather than an organizational resource. Ashford and Cummings (1983) remind us that when people are given a great deal of feedback by others, they are less likely to seek their own feedback. Information imposed by others tends to increase rather than to reduce uncertainty, and that is counterproductive. Information over which the teacher perceives no control tends to raise anxiety rather than contain it, and that is also counterproductive. The feedback seeker is the person most able to determine what information from what sources will be optimally useful.

For student surveys, the teacher should have a significant role in determining both the form and the content of items. Video- or audiotaping services should ensure that the tape becomes the property of the teacher. They should include a pretaping conference for the teacher to decide such issues as what the camera will focus on. And they should provide printed advice about using video feedback and suggest colleagues or consultants who can assist with tape analysis. Interviews with students should be construed as the teacher's inquiry into how learning comes about, rather than as assessments of the goodness or badness of the course or the teacher. Interview questions should incorporate suggestions from the teacher, and the teacher should conduct at least some of the interviews.

Faculty-Centered Reflection on Standards. Only rarely do academics directly and sincerely discuss their values about teaching and learning. Rather than collude in this silence, those of us in faculty development should plan dialogues in which values are revealed and confronted. Our role is to articulate positions that provoke responses, to expose contradictions that need attention, and to champion the underdog (usually students) while affirming core academic values. These dialogues require the kind of intellectual labor that academics love and at which they excel, but which they usually reserve for scholarly issues. We may serve as provocateurs, but the direction of dialogues as well as the answers finally attained are determined by faculty.

Faculty-Centered Skill Learning. Some faculty undeniably need skill training, and some even desire it, but this may be the least urgent component of the feedback model. Needs for information (input) and for reflection (standards) are, I believe, even greater. Training on lecturing clearly, conducting discussions wisely, and assessing learning accurately should be available for faculty who request it, but many are already skillful enough to do things differently once they have identified their new intentions. Two skills, however, are not likely to take care of themselves: the skill of deriving new intentions from the conversation between information and standards and the skill of maintaining the intended behaviors.

To refine the skill of identifying behavioral intentions, we should devise occasions where faculty share their new intentions with one another and describe how they have arrived at them. When that is done with care, the change process becomes explicit and replicable. Maintenance of new behaviors over time is difficult in the harried real world of teaching, but we can share devices that provide reminders of these skills, strategies that make the teacher accountable to others who monitor progress, and exercises that anticipate circumstances where the risk of relapse is high (Marx and Karren, 1988; Walton, 1989). Such activities keep faculty at the center and in control. They facilitate rather than inhibit natural tendencies to seek feedback.

Most writings about college teaching and its improvement reflect the perspectives of researchers, consultants, and specialists in professional development. In this chapter, I have written from the faculty's perspective, taking into account the real-world circumstances of academic life, as well as research and theory about effective teaching. My hope is that readers have become more sensitive to factors that influence faculty's openness to change and improvement. Such sensitivity can lead to improvements in the match between programs for evaluation and development and the real world of college teaching.

References

Angelo, T. A. "Faculty Development *for* Learning." In S. Kahn (ed.), *To Improve the Academy: Resources for Student, Faculty, and Institutional Development.* Vol. 8. Stillwater, Okla.: POD and New Forums Press, 1989.

Ashford, S. J., and Cummings, L. L. "Feedback as an Individual Resource: Personal Strategies of Creating Information." *Organizational Behavior and Human Performance,* 1983, 32, 370–398.

Braskamp, L. A., Fowler, D. L., and Ory, J. C. "Faculty Uses of Evaluative Information." Paper presented to the Evaluation Research Society, 1981.

Braskamp, L. A., Fowler, D. L., and Ory, J. C. "Faculty Development and Achievement: A Faculty's View." *Review of Higher Education,* 1984, 7, 205–222.

Cross, K. P., and Angelo, T. A. *The Classroom Research Project: Results at the Three-Quarters Mark.* Berkeley, Calif.: Classroom Research Project, 1989.

Eble, K. E. *The Aims of College Teaching.* San Francisco: Jossey-Bass, 1983.

Epstein, J. (ed.). *Masters: Portraits of Great Teachers.* New York: Basic Books, 1981.

Fox, D. "Personal Theories of Teaching." *Studies in Higher Education,* 1983, *8,* 141–163.

Franklin, J., and Theall, M. "Who Reads Ratings: Knowledge, Attitudes, and Practices of Users of Student Ratings of Instruction." Paper presented at the 73rd annual meetings of the American Educational Research Association, San Francisco, April 1989.

Gmelch, W. H., Lovrich, N. P., and Wilke, P. K. "Sources of Stress in Academe: A National Perspective." *Research in Higher Education,* 1984, *20,* 477–490.

Hoffmann, J., and Oseroff-Varnell, D. "Teacher Effectiveness and Student Ratings: Finding the Missing Link." Paper presented at the 2nd National Conference on the Training and Employment of Teaching Assistants, Seattle, Washington, November 1989.

Maehr, M. L., and Braskamp, L. A. *The Motivation Factor: A Theory of Personal Investment.* Lexington, Mass.: Heath, 1986.

Marx, R. D., and Karren, R. "The Effects of Relapse Prevention Training and Interactive Follow-up on Positive Transfer of Training." Paper presented at the 48th annual meetings of the Academy of Management, Anaheim, California, August 1988.

Menges, R. J. "Applications of Cybernetics and Control Theory to Instructional Consultation in Postsecondary Education." Paper presented at the 71st annual meetings of the American Educational Research Association, Washington, D.C., April 1987.

Menges, R. J., and Brinko, K. T. "Effects of Student Evaluation Feedback: A Meta-Analysis of Higher Education Research." Paper presented at the 70th annual meetings of the American Educational Research Association, San Francisco, April 1986. (ED 270 408)

Menges, R. J., and Rando, W. C. "What Are Your Assumptions? Improving Instruction by Examining Theories." *College Teaching,* 1989, *37* (2), 54–60.

Mooney, C. J. "Professors Are Upbeat About Profession but Uneasy About Students, Standards." *Chronicle of Higher Education,* Nov. 8, 1989, pp. A1, A18–A21.

Murray, H. G. "Impact of Student Instructional Ratings on Quality of Teaching in Higher Education." Paper presented at the 71st annual meetings of the American Educational Research Association, Washington, D.C., April 1987.

Ory, J. C., and Braskamp, L. A. "Faculty Perceptions of the Quality and Usefulness of Three Types of Evaluative Information." *Research in Higher Education,* 1981, *15,* 217–282.

Peterson, P. L., and Comeaux, M. A. "Teachers' Schemata for Classroom Events: The Mental Scaffolding of Teachers' Thoughts During Classroom Instruction." *Teaching and Teacher Education,* 1987, *3,* 319–331.

Povlacs, J. T. "So You've Got Them in Your Office—Now What?" In K. G. Lewis (ed.), *Face to Face: A Sourcebook of Individual Consultation Techniques for Faculty/Instructional Developers.* Stillwater, Okla.: New Forums Press, 1988.

Shaeffer, J. M., McGill, L. T., and Menges, R. J. "Graduate Teaching Assistants' Views on Teaching." In S. Kahn (ed.), *To Improve the Academy: Resources for Student, Faculty, and Institutional Development.* Vol. 8. Stillwater, Okla.: POD and New Forums Press, 1989.

Snyder, M. "Self-Monitoring Processes." *Advances in Experimental Social Psychology,* 1979, *12,* 85–128.

Stark, J. S., Lowther, M. M., Bentley, R. J., and Martens, G. G. "Disciplinary Differences in Course Planning." *Review of Higher Education,* 1990, *13,* 141–165.

Stevens, E. "Tinkering with Teaching." *Review of Higher Education,* 1988, *12,* 63–78.

Tiberius, R. G. "Metaphors Underlying the Improvement of Teaching and Learning." *British Journal of Educational Technology,* 1986, *17* (2), 144–156.
Walton, J. M. "Self-Reinforcing Behavior Change." *Personnel Journal,* 1989, *68* (10), 64–68.

Robert J. Menges is professor of education and social policy at Northwestern University, Evanston, Illinois, and director of the research program on faculty and instruction of the National Center for Postsecondary Teaching, Learning, and Assessment.

Consultants and clients take on various roles when they engage in discussions about teaching. What interactions take place in these sessions? How effective are these interactions and are there ways to ensure their success?

The Interactions of Teaching Improvement

Kathleen T. Brinko

When trying to improve the quality of their instruction, many faculty seek feedback (Ashford and Cummings, 1983) about their teaching from a peer, colleague, or instructional consultant. In fact, instructional consultation is a vital part of approximately half of faculty development programs (Erickson, 1986).

Several reviews of the literature have advocated consultation as an important part of teaching improvement (Levinson-Rose and Menges, 1981; O'Hanlon and Mortensen, 1980), and empirical studies have found evidence concerning the efficacy of consultation. Cohen (1980) conducted a meta-analysis on the effectiveness of student ratings as a feedback mechanism and found that feedback from student ratings coupled with consultation were more effective than feedback from student ratings alone. When they replicated and updated Cohen's work, Menges and Brinko (1986) found that consultation quadrupled the effect of student rating feedback. However, among individual studies there was great variation in the effectiveness of the consultation, and, unfortunately, the studies do not contain descriptions of the interactions between the consultants and faculty members in sufficient detail to permit determination of the factors that contributed to the variability.

In the past decade there have been several efforts to analyze the interactions within the consultation process (Brinko, 1988, 1990; Orban, 1981; Price, 1976; Rutt, 1979). What these studies have shown is that there is no one way in which university people "consult" with each other, and that no one kind of instructional consultation is more effective than others. However, within this tapestry of consultation are several patterns of behavior that are commonly recognized and shared by instructional consultants.

Phases of Interaction

When a faculty member requests assistance with his or her teaching, the interaction between the instructional consultant and the faculty member generally cycles through four phases: *initial contact, conference, information collection,* and *information review and planning session.* Whether they flow together or whether they occur discretely in time, each phase has a distinct purpose and contributes to the overall success of the endeavor.

The initial contact is the first encounter between the consultant and client. It may be either face to face or over the telephone, but it usually is quite brief. It may be used to broach a problem, to explore availability of appropriate assistance, or to set an appointment to meet for the next phase. If both parties are amenable, this phase may flow into the next phase without any lapse in time.

The second phase, the conference, is an extensive discussion between the consultant and the client. The content of this discussion varies, but usually the consultant attempts to understand the context of the faculty member's teaching situation, including the goals of the course, the types of students in the course, the syllabus, the instructional aids, the problems encountered, and the like. If the faculty member seeks advice based on this conversation, the process may be terminated at this point (for insightful analyses of consultation without feedback, see Price, 1976; Rutt, 1979). If the faculty member has questions that can be answered only by the collection of additional information, the process may continue (see Orban, 1981; Brinko, 1988, 1990).

In the information collection phase, the consultant gathers data that are to be fed back to the client. The kinds of information that the consultant collects are dictated by the questions that the faculty member brings to the conference. For example, questions about presentation style are best answered by a trained observer who systematically evaluates the faculty member's presentation in one or more classes. Questions about the effectiveness of explanations are best answered by students—whether in small group interviews, in written comments, or in achievement tests. On the other hand, questions about congruity between theory and practice are best answered by examining course materials or videotaping teacher-student interaction.

In the fourth phase, the information review and planning session, the consultant shares the collected information with the faculty member. In addition to the problems discussed in the conference, other problems may be identified as the consultant and client review the data. These problems are then diagnosed, and specific solutions are explored.

Because instructional consultation is so labor-intensive, many instructional consultation programs combine an abbreviated version of the conference with the information review and planning session. It is sensible to assume that a condensing of the process will have little impact on consultation effectiveness in some cases, such as when a consultant works with a group of teaching assistants in the same course. However, at this time we have no empirical evidence to support this assumption.

The information review and planning session may be the final phase of the interaction, or it may trigger more interaction between the consultant and client (for several examples of information collection and review techniques, see Cooper, 1982; Lewis, 1988). Figure 3.1 illustrates the four phases of interaction and highlights critical decision points in the instructional consultation process.

The effectiveness of the consultation process is determined by how well the client and consultant utilize the opportunities of each of the four phases. Each phase presents consultants and clients with occasions to

Figure 3.1. Four Phases of Instructional Consultation with Feedback

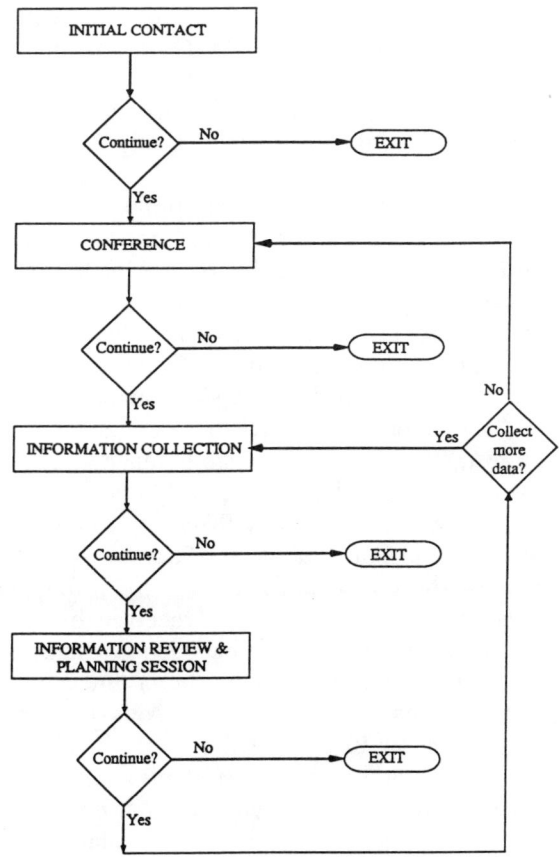

obtain important information about the process and each other, and to make informed decisions based on this knowledge. In each of these phases, consultants and clients assess their compatibility with each other, learn new perspectives about the teaching-learning process, and determine whether instructional consultation will answer the questions at hand. Table 3.1 summarizes the opportunities of each of the four phases.

Models of Interaction

In the education, psychology, and organizational behavior literature, several researchers (Blake and Mouton, 1983; Cash and Minter, 1979; Dalgaard, Simpson, and Carrier, 1982; Davies, 1975; Gallessich, 1974, 1982; Rutt, 1979; Schein, 1969; Tilles, 1961) have proposed models of consultative interaction. Although the names vary, the descriptions of these models are remarkably similar and can be distilled into eight different models of consultative interaction. Using Gallessich's (1974) terminology, these eight models are (1) information transmission, (2) medical, (3) mental health, (4) program consultation and implementation, (5) process consultation, (6) advocacy consultation, and, using Blake and Mouton's (1983) terminology, (7) acceptant and (8) confrontation. These models are compared in Table 3.2.

When considering the special case of instructional consultation, four of these models appear to be the most useful. Using Rutt's (1979) terminology, these four models are product, prescription, collaborative/process, and affiliative. Each model typifies a different philosophy and set of expectations that influence the interactions between consultant and client.

Product Model. Consultants and clients working in the product model view the consultant's role as "expert" and the client's role as "seeker of expertise." Before even approaching the consultant, the client identifies and diagnoses the problem and chooses a solution. The client then engages the expertise of the consultant to produce the solution. Sometimes the solution is expertise about "how to" or "the best way to," but often the solution is expertise to produce a test, slide show, video, lab manual, or other product that can remediate the problem. In effect, the client "purchases" what the consultant has "for sale" (Schein, 1969; Tilles, 1961).

Prescription Model. Consultants and clients working in the prescription model view the consultant's role as "identifier, diagnoser, and solver of problems" and the client's role as "receiver thereof." Also known as the medical model, the relationship between consultant and client is much like the 1950s relationship between doctor and patient (Gallessich, 1974; Schein, 1969; Tilles, 1961). Only the consultant possesses valid opinions or knowledge about instructional matters; the client accepts those opinions or knowledge without question. Thus, the prescription client may describe his or her concerns about teaching, but the consultant assumes authority and responsibility for identifying, diagnosing, and solving

Table 3.1. Four Phases of Instructional Consultation with Feedback and Their Opportunities for Consultant and Client

Consultant Opportunities	Client Opportunities
Initial Contact	
Get a first impression of client	Get a first impression of consultant
Establish the reason for consultation	Convey the reason for contact
Set an appointment for a conference	Determine the desirability of consultation
	Reduce feelings of isolation in teaching
Conference	
Establish rapport with the client	Establish rapport with consultant
Analyze the client's teaching situation	Receive another perspective
Determine the client's philosophical and professional orientations	Determine consultant's philosophical and professional orientations
Make a written or verbal contract with client regarding timetable, type of information to be collected, preliminary goals, problems in the client's teaching	Make a written or verbal contract with consultant regarding timetable, type of information to be collected, preliminary goals, problems in client's teaching
Make a verbal or psychological contract with the client regarding expectations, assumptions	Make a verbal or psychological contract with consultant regarding expectations, assumptions
Information Collection	
Systematically gather information about teaching performance	
Information Review and Planning Session	
Convey information gathered about teaching performance	Receive systematically collected information about teaching performance
Offer interpretations of the information collected	Offer interpretations of the information collected
Suggest alternative behaviors or strategies for change	Choose alternative behaviors or strategies for change
Assist in decision making	Receive support for decisions made
Provide support for decisions made	Decide whether further assistance is desirable
Offer further assistance	Determine the effectiveness of the process

Table 3.2. Comparison of Models of Consultation, by Discipline

School Psychology	Organizational Behavior			Education		
Gallessich, 1974	Blake and Mouton, 1983	Tilles, 1961	Schein, 1969	Davies, 1975	Rutt, 1979	Dalgaard, Simpson, and Carrier, 1982
1. Information transmission	Theory principles	Purchase-Sale	Purchase	Product oriented	Product	Consultant as expert
2. Medical	Prescriptive	Doctor-Patient	Doctor-Patient	Prescription oriented	Prescription	Consultant as problem solver
3. Mental health						
4. Program consultation and implementation						
5. Process consultation	Catalytic	Constructive	Process	Product-Process	Collaborative/Process	Consultant as collaborator
6. Advocacy consultation						
7.	Acceptant				Affiliative	Consultant as counselor
8.	Confrontation					

problems—which may or may not be related to the concerns expressed by the client.

Collaborative/Process Model. Consultants and clients working in the collaborative/process model view the consultant's role as "catalyst" or "facilitator of change" and the client's role as "content expert" (Blake and Mouton, 1983; Dalgaard, Simpson, and Carrier, 1982). Collaborative consultants and clients are partners, each having some unique expertise to contribute to the teaching improvement process. Proponents of collaborative consultation believe that such a synergistic relationship produces a result that is far better than what each person working alone may be able to produce. Both the consultant and client may identify, diagnose, and suggest solutions to problems; however, it is the client's prerogative to accept or reject the consultant's contributions. Unlike the prescription model, the client retains authority and responsibility for the process and its results.

Affiliative Model. Consultants and clients working in the affiliative model view the consultant's role as a combination of instructional consultant and psychological counselor and the client's role as seeker of personal as well as professional growth (Andrews, 1978; Dalgaard, Simpson, and Carrier, 1982). Affiliative consultants focus on empowering the client and solving personal problems that may cause or exacerbate the client's instructional problems. The client identifies and diagnoses problems, and the consultant accepts these perceptions (Blake and Mouton, 1983). Like the collaborative model, both the consultant and client may suggest solutions, but it is the client who retains control of the process. Although it is not a common approach to instructional consultation (Brinko, 1988), the affiliative model has been used successfully to improve teaching (Andrews, 1978).

Confrontational Model. A fifth model that has not been suggested previously as a viable alternative in instructional consultation is the confrontational model (Blake and Mouton, 1983). In this model, the consultant takes the role of "challenger" or "devil's advocate," which coerces the client into the role of either defender or accepter. The consultant and client may begin the consultation process using either the collaborative or the affiliative model, but at some point the consultant recognizes that the problem is different from that identified by the client. Perhaps the client is denying the problem or is personally or professionally threatened by it. Thus, to bring about any meaningful change, the consultant feels a need to confront the client as a first step in solving the problem.

While the confrontational model is not currently recognized in the instructional consultation literature, it has potential for facilitating change with some faculty. For example, I wonder whether the result achieved would have been different had the confrontational model been used with a particular faculty client in a previous study (Brinko, 1988). In the beginning of the information review and planning session, the consultant working with this faculty member used a very prescriptive style, authoritatively yet kindly setting the agenda and reviewing the gathered information. But after five minutes of this style of interaction, the client seized control and continued to control the conversation for the remainder of the meeting. For the next forty-five minutes, this instructor quickly and repeatedly interrupted and rebuffed the consultant when he offered his observations and opinions. This faculty member assumed no responsibility for any of his instructional problems and insisted that they resulted from his students' unwillingness to learn, laziness, and irresponsibility. It became clear to this consultant (and to me as the researcher) that this faculty member had no desire to change any of his teaching attitudes or practices. Toward the middle of the session, the consultant abandoned his prescriptive model and adopted the collaborative model, accepting the client's interpretation of events. Undoubtedly, the client left with what he had come for: a validated perspective about his teaching and a certificate of participation for purposes of promotion, tenure, and merit. But it would be difficult by any standard to call this consultation a success. Had the consultant challenged, rather than accepted, the client's negative attitudes and assumptions about his students, some positive change may have been effected in this instructor's behavior. In this case, the confrontational model may have proved to be a useful tool had the consultant been able and willing to use it.

Dynamics of Consultative Interaction

Many researchers maintain that consultative interaction must be client-centered and collaborative if it is to be useful to the client and if it is to be effective in producing behavior change (Carroll and Goldberg, 1989; Cooper, 1982; Dalgaard, Simpson, and Carrier, 1982; Orban, 1981; Sweeney and Grasha, 1979). However, as the above example illustrates, an accepting and collaborative consultant may not be effective for all clients all of the time.

Many practicing consultants recognize the need for more than one type of consultative interaction (Blake and Mouton, 1983; Gallessich, 1974; Schein, 1969; Tilles, 1961). In their experience as instructional consultants, Wergin, Mason, and Munson (1976) reported that their roles shifted from "experts" to "collaborators" as their relationship matured with the client and as the client developed more teaching expertise. When consulting with novice teachers, these consultants felt the need to be more directive and didactic until the client's knowledge base about teaching was expanded; thus their interactions with novice teachers focused on expert and professional information. Also, early in their relationships with clients, these consultants felt the need to establish trust and credibility; thus consultative interactions with new clients also focused on expert and professional information. However, when the faculty member became better acquainted with either pedagogy or the consultant, consultative interactions reportedly became more personal and collaborative.

Like Wergin, Mason, and Munson (1976), consultants in another study (Brinko, 1988) reported that they were more likely to be prescriptive with new clients and more likely to be collaborative with returning clients. However, their reported behavior differed greatly from their observed behavior. The consultative style of these consultants ranged from very prescriptive to very collaborative, with both new and returning clients. In addition, neither gender, training, nor experience as a consultant correlated with consultative style.

These mixed results indicate that consultative interaction cannot be predicted simply by demographics; any model of consultative interaction can emerge depending on the dynamics between consultant and client. Consultant behavior is greatly influenced by client behavior, and, in turn, client behavior is greatly influenced by consultant behavior. In my earlier example, the overbearing and controlling client's behavior greatly influenced—if not caused—the consultant to change his approach to the consultation. Another consultant in the same study effectively used a collaborative style, accepting his client's problem identifications, diagnoses, and solutions; but this consultation apparently succeeded because the client seemed very willing to examine his teaching honestly, to recognize errors and problem areas, and to be receptive to change. A third consultant in that study, who was collaborative almost to the point of being passive, well complemented an assertive, self-analyzing client. However, had this same self-knowledgeable client encountered a highly prescriptive consultant, the mismatch of styles could have seriously impeded the success of the consultation.

Future Directions

The above examples point to the need to consider the interactive style of the consultant-client dyad as a whole. Rather than the consultant's style of interaction, instructional consultation practitioners and researchers need to consider the consultative style that emerges from the interaction between the consultant and the client.

Practitioners who use only one style of consultation focus on their own needs (for example, a need for control or approval) and neglect the needs and expectations of their clients. Thus, the use of only one style of instructional consultation with all clients can affect the success of the consultation and can diminish the satisfaction of clients who have different styles of interaction. Practitioners can meet the needs of a greater number of clients with one of two strategies. In the first strategy, the consultant discusses the client's expectations, is responsive to the client's wishes and cues, and is flexible in his interactional style. This method may be effective for the consultant who possesses a repertoire of consultation models and is comfortable switching back and forth among them. In the second strategy, the consultant discusses her own consultative style and expectations and presents the client with the option of consulting with her. This method may be effective for the instructional consultant who has one particular model in which she has expertise. Both methods are proactive, turning the psychological contract into a verbal contract. Each strategy helps consultants to minimize their assumptions and inferences about clients and to make consistent their espoused theories and theories-in-use (Smith and Schwartz, 1985).

Although there is some agreement in the literature about consultant attitudes and behaviors in general that contribute to effective consultation, we still have no empirical evidence to differentiate between strategies and practices that make consultation successful and those that do not. Researchers need to compare successful and unsuccessful consultation, as defined by the consultant and client, to determine which practices are effective, with whom they are effective, and under what conditions they are effective.

References

Andrews, J.D.W. "Growth of a Teacher." *Journal of Higher Education,* 1978, *49,* 136–150.

Ashford, S. J., and Cummings, L. L. "Feedback as an Individual Resource: Personal Strategies of Creating Information." *Organizational Behavior and Human Performance,* 1983, *32,* 370–398.

Blake, R. R., and Mouton, J. S. *Consultation: A Handbook for Individual and Organization Development.* Reading, Mass.: Addison-Wesley, 1983.

Brinko, K. T. "Instructional Consultation with Feedback in Higher Education: A Quantitative and Qualitative Analysis." *Dissertation Abstracts International,* 1988, *49* (8), 2120A–2121A. (University Microfilms No. 8822955)

Brinko, K. T. "Instructional Consultation with Feedback in Higher Education." *Journal of Higher Education,* 1990, *61,* 65–83.

Carroll, J. G., and Goldberg, S. R. "Teaching Consultants: A Collegial Approach to Better Teaching." *College Teaching,* 1989, *37,* 143–146.

Cash, W. B., and Minter, R. L. "Consulting Approaches: Two Basic Styles." *Training and Development Journal,* 1979, *33,* 26–28.

Cohen, P. A. "Effectiveness of Student-Rating Feedback for Improving College Instruction: A Meta-Analysis of Findings." *Research in Higher Education,* 1980, *13* (4), 321–341.

Cooper, C. R. "Getting Inside the Instructional Process: A Collaborative Diagnostic Process for Improving College Teaching." *Journal of Instructional Development,* 1985, *5* (3), 2–10.

Dalgaard, K. A., Simpson, D. E., and Carrier, C. A. "Coordinate Status Consultation: A Strategy for Instructional Improvement." *Journal of Instructional Development,* 1982, *5* (4), 7–14.

Davies, I. K. "Some Aspects of a Theory of Advice: The Management of an Instructional Developer-Client, Evaluator-Client Relationship." *Instructional Science,* 1975, *3,* 351–373.

Erickson, G. R. "A Survey of Faculty Development Practices." In M. Svinicki, J. Kurfiss, and J. Stone (eds.), *To Improve the Academy: Resources for Student, Faculty, and Institutional Development.* Vol. 5. Stillwater, Okla.: POD and New Forums Press, 1986.

Gallessich, J. "Training the School Psychologist for Consultation." *Journal of School Psychology,* 1974, *12,* 138-149.

Gallessich, J. *The Profession and Practice of Consultation: A Handbook for Consultants, Trainers of Consultants, and Consumers of Consultation Services.* San Francisco: Jossey-Bass, 1982.

Levinson-Rose, J., and Menges, R. J. "Improving College Teaching: A Critical Review of Research." *Review of Educational Research,* 1981, *51,* 403-434.

Lewis, K. G. (ed.). *Face to Face: A Sourcebook of Individual Consultation Techniques for Faculty/Instructional Developers.* Stillwater, Okla.: New Forums Press, 1988.

Menges, R. J., and Brinko, K. T. "Effects of Student Evaluation Feedback: A Meta-Analysis of Higher Education Research." Paper presented at the 70th annual meetings of the American Educational Research Association, San Francisco, April 1986. (ED 270 408)

O'Hanlon, J., and Mortensen, L. "Making Teacher Evaluation Work." *Journal of Higher Education,* 1980, *51,* 664-672.

Orban, D. A. "An Ethnographic Study of Consultation to Improve College Instruction." *Dissertation Abstracts International,* 1981, *42,* 5040A. (University Microfilms No. DA8212435)

Price, R. D. "A Description of the Verbal Behavior of Selected Instructional Developers in Their Initial Conference with New Clients: An Exploratory Study." *Dissertation Abstracts International,* 1976, *37* (9), 5576A.

Rutt, D. P. "An Investigation of the Consultation Styles of Instructional Developers." *Dissertation Abstracts International,* 1979, *40* (2), 624A.

Schein, E. H. *Process Consultation: Its Role in Organization Development.* Reading, Mass.: Addison-Wesley, 1969.

Smith, R. A., and Schwartz, F. S. "A Theory of Effectiveness." In J. R. Jeffrey and G. R. Erickson (eds.), *To Improve the Academy: Resources for Student, Faculty, and Institutional Development.* Vol. 4. Stillwater, Okla.: POD and New Forums Press, 1985.

Sweeney, J. M., and Grasha, A. F. "Improving Teaching Through Faculty Development Triads." *Educational Technology,* 1979, *12* (2), 54-57.

Tilles, S. "Understanding the Consultant's Role." *Harvard Business Review,* 1961, *39,* 87-89.

Wergin, J. F., Mason, E. J., and Munson, P. J. "The Practice of Faculty Development: An Experience-Derived Model." *Journal of Higher Education,* 1976, *47,* 289-308.

Kathleen T. Brinko is coordinator of faculty and academic development in the Hubbard Center for Faculty Development and Instructional Services at Appalachian State University, Boone, North Carolina.

PART TWO

Data for Teaching Improvement

Merely conducting an assessment does not guarantee improvement. Improvement occurs when instructors, students, and others use data gathered through a comprehensive process to understand teaching and learning and to make well-informed decisions about instructional development.

Using Assessment Data to Improve Teaching

Peter J. Gray

Assessment has been described in two different ways. One is a very narrow description that specifies what assessment should focus on (student outcomes) and why assessment should be conducted (for the purpose of program accountability). While this description directs our attention to program effects, the problem is that it has done little to enlighten our understanding of why teaching is effective or how it can be improved. Another problem with describing assessment in terms of a single focus (student outcomes) and a single purpose (accountability) is that assessment can easily become equated with a narrow set of means for holding people and programs accountable, that is, the measurement of student outcomes through standardized, norm-referenced student testing. As a result, confusion arises, since it is unclear whether assessment is a goal (accountability) or an activity (student testing). To the extent that this confusion has occurred within the current assessment movement, it has led some to suggest that the means have replaced the ends (White, 1990) and others to warn against the pitfalls in studying student outcomes (Terenzini, 1989). Such concerns have stimulated authors such as Ewell (1991) to describe new forms of assessment in higher education. This tension between means and ends brings us to the second way of describing assessment. This description concerns assessment as a process that is analogous to other applied research processes such as educational evaluation.

A Current Approach to Assessment

Well-established processes such as evaluation research can inform the design and implementation of assessments, as illustrated by Gray (1989b).

Other sources such as Erwin (1991, p. xv) provide guidance "for those who collect, review, use, and submit evidence about the strengths and weaknesses of their educational programs."

As the assessment movement matured over the last decade, the prevailing description changed from a limited, short-term focus on measurement of student outcomes to a much broader, long-term focus on a range of techniques used to gather a variety of information in support of instructional, programmatic, and institutional change. As Marchese (1987, p. 8) suggested, "Assessment per se guarantees nothing by way of improvement. . . . Only when used in combination with good instruction . . . in a program of improvement, can the device strengthen education."

This broader definition of assessment guides the discussion in this chapter because the focus here is on gathering information for the purposes of understanding and improving teaching as well as judging its quality. In familiar evaluation terms, the purposes are both formative and summative. As in the design and development of any formative or summative evaluation, the instructor (or project team) should ask and answer the following questions: What are the purpose and focus of the assessment? Who will use the results of the assessment? What questions guide the assessment? What data should be collected to answer these questions? What is the plan for data collection, analysis, summary, and reporting? Each of these questions has many possible answers, and because these answers provide the context for the assessment, they must be complete.

Assessing the Components of Teaching

Teaching is an activity that has three essential components: content, process, and impact. Assessment should gather information about all three components, and the process of assessing the effectiveness of instruction should be flexible because the situations and contexts of teaching are extremely varied. Consider, for example, the following list of factors that can influence the ways in which instructors plan their courses (adapted from Geis and Hiscock, 1991): knowledge and skill of instructor and students, unique needs of the discipline, level of students and the instruction, instructors' experience, delivery mode, departmental guidelines and instructor control, environment and resources, incentive systems and student motivation, and perceived roles. Geis and Hiscock (1991, p. 2) suggest that many improvement efforts may be "missing the mark" because faculty approach course design and planning in "an intuitive and highly personal way" whereas instructional designers rely on "the systematic (and proven successful) instructional design heuristic."

With respect to the five questions asked earlier about the design and development of an evaluation, the assessment would have to weigh the potential influence of the factors listed above in order to contribute to a sound decision about which questions to ask and how to collect data. Even when faculty members are concerned only with the improvement of instruction in their own courses, it is still worthwhile to think about the entire instructional design and development process, since various courses will be at different points in the process at any given time. Taking these factors into consideration, the task of instructional design and development is to select the right topics, at appropriate levels of sophistication for the students involved, and to match them with the most effective and efficient methods and technologies in order to produce the desired student learning. Assessment plays a crucial role in this process.

In the following discussion, the specific purposes and focus of assessment are related to certain stages in the instructional design and development process where data are collected, used, and reported. The assumption is that the overarching goal of assessment is to support either instructional self-improvement by an individual instructor or course and curriculum change by a group of people. Figure 4.1 provides an overall view of course, curriculum, and program development data. Figure 4.2 isolates three stages of the design and development process (problem clarification, design/redesign, and field testing and implementation) and identifies four areas of concentration for each stage (audiences, questions, data, and assessment plan). In the following sections, each stage is discussed with respect to the four areas of concentration.

Figure 4.1. Course, Curriculum, and Program Development Data

```
┌─────────────┐      ┌─────────────┐
│  Problem    │      │   Basic     │
│Clarification│─────▶│   Input     │
│    Data     │      │    Data     │
└─────────────┘      └─────────────┘
       │                    │
       ▼                    ▼
┌─────────────┐   ┌─────────────┐   ┌──────────────┐   ┌────────────────┐
│   Project   │──▶│   Design    │──▶│ Field Testing│──▶│ Implementation │
│  Selection  │   │     or      │   │              │   │                │
│             │   │  Redesign   │   │              │   │                │
└─────────────┘   └─────────────┘   └──────────────┘   └────────────────┘
                                       ↘    ↗              ↘    ↗
                                    ┌──────────┐        ┌──────────┐
                                    │ Data On: │        │ Data On: │
                                    │ • Plans  │        │ • Impact │
                                    │ • Use    │        │ • Procedures │
                                    │ • Outcomes│       │          │
                                    └──────────┘        └──────────┘
                                                           ➥ Reporting
```

Source: Gray and Diamond, 1989.

Figure 4.2. Design/Development Stages and Assessment Areas of Concentration

Stages	Areas
• Problem Clarification	• Audiences
• Design/Redesign	• Questions
• Field Testing and Implementation	• Data
	• Assessment Plan

Stage 1: Problem Clarification

Faculty members have many demands on their time and energy. Therefore, they need sound information to determine if an instructional or course development project is worth considering. The initial motivation to consider instructional improvement may come from a vague sense of uneasiness about the way things are going or from a very concrete indication that things are not going well. The stimulus for change may come from the faculty member, students or their parents, other faculty and administrators, or alumni and employers off-campus. Whether or not there is specific evidence that a problem exists, one should begin by being clear about the extent and causes of perceived or real problems related to the need for instructional change. That is the purpose of assessment in the first stage of the instructional improvement process.

Audiences. Potential audiences for the results of the assessment include the instructor, a project team, other faculty, students, the department chair and other administrators, alumni, professionals in the field, and employers off-campus. In fact, the audience can include anyone who would be affected by the instructional change.

Questions. As noted above, there are questions about instructional content, process, and impact at each stage. Sudweeks and Diamond (1980), Braskamp, Brandenburg, and Ory (1984), and Seldin (1984), among others, provide extensive lists of topics that should be considered in the initial assessment of a course. In regard to problem clarification, the questions all concern the current situation. There may be questions about what is being taught, that is, whether the goals and objectives of the instruction are appropriate for the students in terms of their background and experience, whether the course fits into the curriculum, and whether its syllabus is up to date in terms of the topics and sophistication of its content.

There also may be questions about the efficiency and effectiveness of the instructional process, that is, whether the methods and technologies are effective, enjoyable, and motivating, whether the instructional process facilitates student learning of the course content, and whether this learning contributes to students' success in other courses or after they graduate. Similarly, there may be questions about student effort, that is, how motivated and conscientious the students are relative to learning the course content.

Another set of relevant questions to ask at this stage concerns the potential for success of an instructional change project. These questions have to do with political and organizational issues as they influence the relative merit of expending one's energy on such a project in light of other pressing needs. Diamond (1989) provides a thorough description of some of these issues. For example, some questions may concern stability in the department and curriculum, that is, whether the faculty, the administration, or the curriculum of the department is likely to change in a way that adversely affects the improvement effort. Other questions may concern the potential support for an improvement effort in terms of resources and rewards. Support might be in the form of an adequate timeline, a reduced load, a teaching or research assistant, funds for travel, materials, or equipment, and salary increments based on successful completion of the project. Still other questions may concern the perceived importance of the project in the department; in the school, college, or university; or on the national scene, in a specific discipline or in society in general.

We should not ask only one type of question because we will get only a partial answer to the larger question of the underlying need for instructional change. However, at this stage, an extensive study need not be undertaken. The depth of the assessment should be sufficient to make a decision about whether an instructional design or redesign project is worthwhile.

Data. When describing the data to be collected, both the source and type of data should be specified. For example, students' grades in a particular course and in other related courses might be identified as useful information in answering questions about impact or lack thereof. However, to fully understand the significance of these grades, data should be gathered from faculty in the department about the integration of the course into the total curriculum, from students about the perceived value of the course content, and from the instructor regarding student effort.

Information about the potential for success is somewhat harder to come by. It may be provided by the department chair or other senior faculty, but it does not necessarily have to be in the form of black-and-white statements. Instead, a project's potential for success may be communicated through informal conversations with a department chair about the relative priority of a particular effort or the likelihood and extent of the resources that may be provided. The potential for success might also be communicated by the amount of time that faculty and others are willing to spend on the project, for example, in informal conversations or as part of a formal departmental meeting agenda. On the other hand, there may be specific policies regarding rewards for instructional improvement efforts, or instructional improvement grant programs may be available for additional support.

Assessment Plan. How and when these data are collected, analyzed, summarized, and reported will vary extensively. If the information to be collected already exists in one form or another, this first stage will take about one semester. For example, reviews of existing student records regarding grades, registration and withdrawal patterns, standardized test scores, and course evaluation surveys can help to determine student impact, student perceptions of the course's value, and student effort. Content analysis of the course syllabus and materials by knowledgeable professionals can help answer questions about the appropriateness of the course content and its fit within the larger curriculum. If critical data are not readily available, then this stage can take longer, since a means of collecting new data must be developed and implemented.

The time frame and procedures for gathering information about the potential for success are also more difficult to specify than are those for explicating the need for instructional improvement. The procedures may include informal conversations with key faculty and administrators, review of policy statements, or development of grant proposals. The determination of the potential for success, if not the actual guarantee, should also take about a semester.

Other important parts of the assessment plan are the analysis, summary, and reporting of results. If the instructor is the primary recipient of the assessment results, then this aspect can be fairly informal; that is, hand-calculated frequency counts of survey item responses, first-hand review of existing records, or open-ended comments may be sufficient. However, if the assessment is intended to help a department or larger unit decide whether or not to proceed with a major course or curriculum development project, then professional assistance should be sought for the statistical analysis of quantitative data about enrollment over time, students' grades, and course ratings, and for the textual analysis of narrative comments on surveys, course syllabi, and instructional materials. The analysis, summary, and reporting of data should be organized by the questions that guided the assessment and should be implemented in a way that provides meaningful and understandable information to the key audiences, that is, those who will decide if an instructional improvement project is warranted.

Stage 2: Design or Redesign

In the second stage, the collection of basic data provides the information needed to design or redesign instruction, including the production and development of instructional and other support materials. To some extent the information collected during the first stage should be useful in answering the assessment questions at the second stage. That is, the specific purpose and focus of the assessment at stage 2 depends on what was discovered about the extent and causes of perceived or real problems related to the content, process, and impact of instruction. However, the assessment at stage 2 goes into more depth in order to identify the content of instruction as well as its likely impact on achievement of instructional goals and objectives. The description of process concerns the methods and technologies used with the particular materials, equipment, and techniques of instruction intended to accomplish the goals and objectives.

Audiences. The audiences for the assessment at stage 2 are determined by the extent of the design or redesign project and can range in scope from a single instructor initiating a change in a course to many different on-campus and off-campus groups involved in a curriculum project. The audiences of the assessment are, in effect, those who will make decisions about the design or redesign of instruction. Therefore, knowledge about who they are, their questions, and their preferences regarding data helps to determine the procedures for collecting, analyzing, summarizing, and reporting the data, which, in turn, increases the potential for effective use of the assessment results.

Questions. There are two major sets of questions at the second stage. One set helps to create the ideal design or redesign, and the other set provides direction for reconciling this ideal with the realities of the context of instruction. The task of creating the ideal instruction raises questions about the domain of knowledge and the specific content, that is, the desired or essential goals and objectives of instruction. The following types of questions (adapted from Diamond, 1989) bear on this issue: (1) Questions regarding ideal instruction concern ideal students. Students should be described in such diverse terms as their academic backgrounds and experiences (related to their respective entrance levels of competence and their ability to meet prerequisites), their specific reasons for enrolling, their long-term personal and career-related goals, their general attitudes about the discipline, and their specific assumptions about the instructional content and the course or program in question. (2) Questions related to ideal instruction also concern societal issues such as how the instruction helps students acquire basic competencies, how it can better prepare students for jobs, further education, and so on, and how it can help accomplish the mission of the program, department, or institution. (3) Questions related to the ideal processes of instruction concern methods and technologies that are proven by pedagogical tradition and research.

Just as there is a set of political and organizational issues related to the efficacy of even engaging in an instructional improvement project, there are similar issues related to the reconciliation of the ideal design or redesign and the realities of a given context. Diamond (1989) also observes that the realities of the situation must be addressed. The following types of questions address these realities: (1) questions about how the specific content of instruction fits into the larger context, for example, any extant discipline requirements such as those necessary for accreditation or any future trends or emerging areas of content in a discipline, (2) questions about the actual students who are likely to be involved in instruction, including their backgrounds and experiences, their motivations, and so on, (3) questions about the amount of time within a program or curriculum that can be allotted to particular instruction; the extent that other instructional resources can be allotted, for example, instructional staff, space, materials, and equipment; and any institutional constraints regarding priorities and finances.

Data. The data needed at stage 2 are often more extensive than those required at stage 1 because they are used not just to decide if a project should take place but also to actually design or redesign instruction, including the development and production of materials and activities. However, it is often possible to build on the information initially collected. For example, data collected at stage 1 on students' backgrounds and experiences and on their current and subsequent grades may point the direction for further investigation of the reality of students' preparation and their levels of motivation and effort. New data will often involve information from students, faculty, and others about what ideally should be the content and process of instruction and what realities must be taken into account, since these are the special concerns in the design or redesign stage.

Assessment Plan. Data collection techniques and the sources of information can be quite varied. Because of the extensive and sophisticated nature of the assessment plans at stage 2, it is advisable to seek support from an individual or an agency on campus such as an instructional development or teaching and learning center, an office of evaluation and research, or a testing services department.

For smaller projects a single semester is probably sufficient for design or redesign and the assessment needed to support this stage, during which the ideal instruction and the real constraints are investigated. Development and production could then take place over the next semester in preparation for field testing the following term. If extensive development and production of materials and activities are necessary, then another semester may be needed to prepare for field testing.

Stage 3: Field Testing and Implementation

Once developed and produced, instructional activities, materials, technologies, and so on need to be field tested before final implementation. Field testing implies an assessment designed to provide information for the refinement of instruction (so-called formative assessment). Implementation implies an assessment designed to determine if instruction is functioning as intended and having the desired impact (so-called summative assessment).

Audiences. The audiences for field testing and implementation assessments also can range from a single instructor to many different on-campus and off-campus groups who will make decisions about the newly designed or redesigned instruction. Different people may be involved in different aspects of the assessment as providers of information and users of information. For example, students may have a role in completing course evaluation surveys as participants in courses, and they may be involved in making decisions about the success of instruction as part of a departmental curriculum revision committee.

Questions. Both formative and summative questions focus on the content, process, and impact of instruction, as well as on the effort of students. However, formative questions are phrased in a more tentative manner and seek to elicit both information about the current situation and suggestions for refinement.

Field testing may take place relative to components of instruction, for example, a single topic, one set of materials or activities, or one course of an entire curriculum. There are a variety of topics on which field testing and implementation assessment questions can focus. These questions can cover content, process, and impact. Each statement incorporates both what should be assessed and the criterion for judging it, for example, stated goals and objectives and their clarity.

Data. The data needed to answer the assessment questions during the field test and implementation stage are as varied as the content, processes, and impact of instruction, and the data collected may include both perceptions and facts. Perceptions concern criteria such as clarity, appropriateness, relevance, effectiveness, and so on. Facts concern the congruence between plans and their implementation and between intended and actual outcomes. Questions at this point are concerned with outcomes; for example, "To what extent do students perceive the course goals and objectives clearly?" "What is the students' level of achievement?" or "In what ways do the anticipated and actual outcomes match?" Of course, if summative questions result in negative answers, then they may suggest the need for improvement, which in turn may raise the issue of whether a new project should be started.

Assessment Plan. Similarly, the means and timing of collecting, analyzing, summarizing, and reporting formative and summative data are extremely varied. Field testing of a single course or set of materials could take place in a semester, and after revisions, implementation could take place the next time the course is offered or the materials are used. The assessment plan in this case could be narrowly focused and brief. At the other extreme, field testing and revision of the various courses in a new curriculum alone could take several years, and it could be five years or more before the entire curriculum is implemented and ready for a summative assessment.

This situation involving long-term processes is supported by case studies of several of the most successful institutional change projects with strong assessment components. The people at Northeast Missouri State University talk about the following stages of change related to the development and adoption of assessment: readiness, implementation, acceptance, and commitment (McClain, Krueger, and Kangas, 1989). For example, at King's College in Wilkes-Barre, Pennsylvania, ten years of planned change have taken place. "Before possible changes in the curriculum were even discussed, five years were spent on faculty development. It was only after an outcome-oriented curriculum had been agreed upon that the concept of assessment was introduced" (Gray, 1989a, p. 4).

Summary

As the assessment movement has matured over the last decade, the prevailing emphasis has changed from a limited, short-term focus on measurement of student outcomes with standardized, norm-referenced tests for the purpose of accountability, to a much broader, long-term focus on a range of techniques designed to gather information for instructional, programmatic, and institutional change. This broader definition of assessment, which is analogous to definitions of other systematic processes such as evaluation research, guided the discussion of instructional improvement in this chapter. Individual family members, either alone or as part of a team, can become involved in a wide range of instructional improvement projects. Assessment plays a crucial support role at each instructional design and development stage: problem clarification, design or redesign, and field testing and implementation. In the next two chapters of Part Two of this volume, specific techniques for collecting and using data are described. These techniques can be used at each stage of the process described here and are valuable tools for both faculty and instructional designers.

References

Braskamp, L. A., Brandenburg, D. C., and Ory, J. C. *Evaluating Teaching Effectiveness.* Newbury Park, Calif.: Sage, 1984.

Diamond, R. M. *Designing and Improving Courses and Curricula in Higher Education: A Systematic Approach.* San Francisco: Jossey-Bass, 1989.

Erwin, T. D. *Assessing Student Learning and Development: A Guide to the Principles, Goals, and Methods of Determining College Outcomes.* San Francisco: Jossey-Bass, 1991.

Ewell, P. T. "To Capture the Ineffable: New Forms of Assessment in Higher Education." In G. Grant (ed.), *Review of Research in Education.* Washington, D.C.: American Educational Research Association, 1991.

Geis, G. L., and Hiscock, P. "How Professors Plan Courses." Paper presented at the 75th annual meetings of the American Educational Research Association, Chicago, April 1991.

Gray, P. J. "Campus Profiles." *Assessment Update,* 1989a, *1* (2), 4–5.

Gray, P. J. (ed.). *Achieving Assessment Goals Using Evaluation Techniques.* New Directions for Higher Education, no. 67. San Francisco: Jossey-Bass, 1989b.

Gray, P. J., and Diamond, R. M. "Improving Higher Education: The Need for a Broad View of Assessment." In P. J. Gray (ed.), *Achieving Assessment Goals Using Evaluation Techniques.* New Directions for Higher Education, no. 67. San Francisco: Jossey-Bass, 1989.

Marchese, T. J. "An Update on Assessment." *AAHE Bulletin,* 1987, *39,* 3–8.

Seldin, P. *Changing Practices in Faculty Evaluation: A Critical Assessment and Recommendations for Improvement.* San Francisco: Jossey-Bass, 1984.

Sudweeks, R., and Diamond, R. M. *Questions That Should Be Considered in Designing a Comprehensive Evaluation of a College Course.* Syracuse, N.Y.: Center for Instructional Development, Syracuse University, 1980.

Terenzini, P. T. "Assessment with Open Eyes: Pitfalls in Studying Student Outcomes." *Journal of Higher Education,* 1989, *60* (6), 644–664.

White, E. M. "Change for the Worse: The Damage of Innovations Set Adrift." *AAHE Bulletin,* 1990, *42,* 3–5.

Peter J. Gray is director of evaluation and research at the Center for Instructional Development, Syracuse University, Syracuse, New York.

The success of teaching improvement efforts often depends on the quality of the information collected by both the faculty member and the instructional/faculty development practitioner. What kinds of information are most usable in teaching improvement and what are some effective ways to collect these data?

Gathering Data for the Improvement of Teaching: What Do I Need and How Do I Get It?

Karron G. Lewis

The phone rings and the instructional consultant from the Center for Teaching Effectiveness answers. It is a faculty member from the Classics Department who has just received the results from last semester's teaching evaluations. In a very distraught tone of voice she says, "The students are all saying the course is terrible and the averages on the scaled items are really low. Can I please make an appointment to discuss this with you?"

The scenario given above is encountered repeatedly as effective teaching is being emphasized at higher education institutions across the country. Although many faculty members say that they distrust student evaluations, the use of these evaluations is becoming more widespread as colleges and universities attempt to cope with the public clamor for improved undergraduate education. Despite this distrust, the results of student evaluations are often the catalyst that encourages faculty members to seek ways to make changes in their teaching methods.

In this chapter we look at the types of data that can inform efforts to improve teaching, the kinds of information provided in each case, and how the data are best presented and used. Although the improvement process is approached from the point of view of a faculty or instructional development practitioner, the same forms, techniques, and other data collection instruments can also be used by individual faculty members who wish to study their own teaching. However, a number of research studies have indicated that improvement in teaching is much more likely if the faculty member works with an experienced consultant rather than alone

(Cohen, 1980; Aleamoni, 1978). Drawing from these studies and his own experience, McKeachie (1987, p. 6) has identified three advantages that collaboration with a consultant can provide to a faculty member:

> First, he or she [the consultant] can help identify particularly important information provided in the data, separating critical information from superficial information. Second, the consultant can provide hope and encouragement. All too often feedback fails because it discourages the individual and increases his or her sense of anxiety and hopelessness. And, third, a consultant can provide suggestions about what to do about the data, for example, suggestions about alternative methods of teaching that may be more productive than those used in the past.

With this model of collaboration between faculty member and experienced consultant in mind, let us return to our faculty member from the Classics Department.

During the initial phone call, the instructional consultant asks the faculty member to gather some preliminary information (student evaluation results, syllabi, exams, textbooks, and so forth) and bring it to their first consultation meeting. Based on the information obtained, the consultant begins making decisions about how to help this particular faculty member. But, what information needs to be collected? What techniques and instruments will yield the most useful data in this particular situation? How can the data be presented to the faculty member in a way that informs as well as motivates her to make necessary changes?

To answer these questions, we first need a working definition of good teaching. Centra's (1987, p. 50) definition is especially astute: "Good teaching occurs when the instructor uses a method that is best suited to his or her abilities and also best suited to accomplishing what the course should accomplish." By defining good teaching in this manner, we are more likely to keep in mind the strengths and weaknesses of the instructor as well as his or her specific goals for the course. This definition also allows us to be creative and look at aspects of the teaching-learning process, including those outside of the "traditional" arena.

Guidelines for Choosing Data Collection Methods and Techniques

To guide our selection of data collection methods and techniques, it is useful at first to distinguish among the "major components of the instructional process and suggest what information is appropriate for diagnosing and strengthening each component" (Menges, 1990, p. 108). Two models describe what typically happens in this process. The first model, proposed by Menges (1990), describes the instructional process as consisting of preconditions, plans, procedures, and products. Although faculty members may not use these same terms to describe the instructional process, Menges's formulation captures what typically takes place when a faculty member is developing a course and using feedback to determine what changes to make the next time it is taught.

The second model is proposed by Weimer (1990). She suggests that there are five steps in the teaching improvement process: step 1—develop instructional awareness, step 2—gather information, step 3—change, make choices, step 4—implement alterations, and step 5—assess effectiveness. Combining the two models, I use the preconditions portion of Menges's model and the first two steps in Weimer's process to guide our selection of the methods and techniques that can be used to gather data.

Phase 1: Exploring Preconditions with the Teacher

Menges (1990, p. 109) defines preconditions as "the circumstances that prevail before any teaching and learning occur." These preconditions include information about subject matter, physical facilities, learners, and teacher. Let us look at the information that we might want to gather under each of these categories.

Subject Matter. How deeply do we, as consultants, look into the whys and wherefores of the courses taught by faculty members who come to us for assistance? Do we ever look at the catalogue descriptions of the courses? Do we try to find out where the courses fall in the curriculum and in a typical student's degree plan? What do other faculty members expect from the courses? Are the courses prerequisites for later upper-division courses? Will the answers to these questions affect the ways that the courses should be taught?

Physical Facilities. If we are going to observe the classes of a faculty member, we typically find out where the class is being held. But do we do any kind of analysis of the physical classroom? What is the layout of the room? How many students will it hold? What is going to be the visual and aural impact on students sitting in the back of the class or on the sides? Will the instructor need a microphone to be heard? What kinds of audio-visual equipment and services are available in that room? Will the answers to these questions affect the way that the course should be taught?

Learners. Typically, when we first talk to a faculty member about his or her concerns, we try to find out a little bit about what the faculty member knows about the students who are taking the course. It is fairly easy to find out how many students there are and, perhaps, what their majors are. What other kinds of information about the students might be useful to know? Why are they taking the course? What are their preferred styles of learning? How have they done in similar courses? How much do they remember from the courses that are prerequisites? Did the instructor administer a pretest to determine their respective levels of understanding of the basics? Will the answers to these questions affect the way that the course should be taught?

Teacher. In our initial interview with the faculty member we try to get a feeling for his or her philosophy of teaching and attitudes toward students. How much time does the instructor devote to teaching—planning, class meetings, and office hours? Does he or she try to interact with students outside of class time and office hours? Will the answers to these questions affect the way that the course should be taught?

Because a faculty member's life is not just what happens on campus or in the classroom, it is also helpful to know something about the faculty member's additional time pressures as well as other work and life priorities: marital status, number of children and their ages, hobbies, outside activities, involvement in professional organizations, and so forth. Some of this information comes out in the initial interview as "small talk" used to make the person feel more comfortable. Nevertheless, knowledge of this kind can shed a great deal of light on why teaching activities might not be going as well as the faculty member would like.

As an example, I had a client from a drama department whose student ratings dropped significantly one semester, although he said that he was doing approximately the same things in class that he had done previously. In our first meeting, he happened to mention that his wife was expecting their second child any day (their first child was four years old). I also discovered that he was program coordinator for the national conference of his professional organization, he was heavily involved in directing several plays (on and off campus), and he was teaching an extra section of one of his classes. By pulling all of this information together and presenting it to him in a time management format, I helped him realize that he actually was not giving nearly as much time and energy to his teaching as he had in previous semesters. Since there was not a great deal that we could do about the workload he had created for himself, we discussed time and stress management techniques and I encouraged him to say no more often during the next semester. Because he was basically a wonderful teacher, his evaluation results were almost back up to normal by the end of the following semester. He said that he had never realized before that "outside" activities could have such an impact on his teaching.

The first kinds of data that consultants need to collect pertain to the current status of these four areas of preconditions. It can also be very beneficial for the instructor to look at and analyze this information. Once consultants have this information about preconditions, then they can move on to focus on the faculty members' concerns about their teaching effectiveness and how to obtain the kinds of information that Weimer (1990) discusses in steps 1 and 2 of her teaching improvement process.

Phase 2: Develop Instructional Awareness

To develop instructional awareness, faculty members need to see themselves as teachers and focus on the things that enhance, and diminish, teacher effectiveness. This means looking closely at themselves and asking questions such as the following: "What do I do when I am in front of the class? Do I pace? Rattle the change in my pocket? Write legibly on the board or overhead? Look at the students when I am talking to them?"

The consultant can help guide this self-analysis by providing checklists, asking questions, videotaping one of the classes, and so forth in order to elicit responses from the faculty member. Methods that can assist faculty members in seeing themselves as their students see them include the following:

Questions and Self-Evaluation Checklists. Weimer, Parrett, and Kerns (1988) provide questions that faculty members can ask themselves as they think about what they do when they are teaching: "What do you do with your hands?" "When do you move?" "Where do you move?" "How do you emphasize main points?" "Do you encourage student participation?" and so forth. By encouraging a faculty member to answer these questions at the beginning of the consultation process, the consultant can help the faculty member focus on specific behaviors. Once these have been identified, the faculty member and the consultant are then able to begin the process of identifying which behaviors are effective and which are not.

Videotape Analysis. A videotape of a faculty member's class can provide another way for him or her to see what kinds of behaviors are used in various situations. This kind of visual record can provide a way for the faculty member to verify the answers that he or she gave to the questions and self-evaluation checklists described above. To guide the viewing of the videotape, additional checklists or other questionnaires can be used. These help focus the faculty member's attention on teaching techniques rather than completely on personal attributes and physical appearance. Often, questionnaires used in videotape analysis ask that the teacher fill out a section prior to viewing the videotape. Forms of this nature thus combine the personal recall of events with what is seen on the videotape, and comparisons can be made. Many faculty members who engage in this process are really surprised when they find that they do not remember many of the details of what happened during their classes.

When a consultant watches videotapes with faculty members, the consultant can help them focus on what they do when they teach and how those behaviors affect student learning (Taylor-Way, 1988). In some faculty/instructional development programs, videotaping is an integral part of individual consultation. In other programs, it is only done if the faculty member indicates that he or she would feel comfortable.

Syllabus. Examination of a course syllabus can help a consultant determine how much time will be spent on each topic, how many exams will be given, what the students' grades will be based on, and even what the instructor wants the students to know and to be able to do when they leave the course. However, a very brief syllabus may provide little information about what to expect. If this is the case, the consultant may need to discuss the syllabus as an "advanced organizer" that helps to create an attitude of expectation among and to motivate the students.

Textbooks. Though textbooks are used in almost all courses in higher education, the selection process is not usually conducted in a methodical manner. By discussing the textbooks selected, the consultant can help a faculty member see them from a student's point of view. Questions such as the following can stimulate discussion: (1) Why was a particular text chosen? "It was the best one available." "It was the one chosen by my predecessor." "Everyone teaching this course uses this book." "It includes most of the topics that I plan to cover." (2) What is the readability level? Researchers tell us that introductory texts should probably be written at the ninth- or tenth-grade level to help student comprehension and motivation (Coil and Bean, 1980). Does the text contain unnecessarily complex language and terminology? Will the student have to have a dictionary in order to read this text? (3) What features of this text will assist student learning? Are there optional workbooks available? What about computer software for drill and practice on factual information?

Readings. Additional readings are frequently cited by students as being too long, difficult to understand, and redundant. As a consultant, I have encountered faculty members who have not recently reread the materials that they are assigning. They may remember this or that item as part of a reading list that they had in graduate school, and that it contained some pertinent information. But they have not timed how long it would take them to read (for comprehension) all of the items assigned.

Redundancy of readings should also be avoided. While it is good to present various viewpoints, multiple readings on one concept or topic may confuse rather than enlighten. If, however, a faculty member takes the time to guide students through several readings, showing them how to find the key points and see the variations among writers, then the students will understand why similar readings are assigned.

Past Exams. Analysis of the formats and cognitive levels of past exams can provide an enormous amount of information about what the faculty member considers important for the students to know and to be able to do when they complete the course. Because many faculty members have not had a course in exam writing prior to acquiring their first college or university position, they often prepare exams that look like those of their favorite teachers in graduate school. These exams may or may not be testing what the faculty member really wants to test or believes is being tested. For example, many multiple-choice exams are written at the cognitive levels of knowledge and comprehension (Bloom, 1972; Lewis, 1982) and thus do not test the students' ability to apply the information or solve problems using the information. This lack of coordination between what is actually learned and what is tested is the primary source of student complaints that exams do not test what they are learning in class.

Other Course Materials. These materials include films, slides, overhead transparencies, handouts, and so forth. They should be carefully chosen or constructed so that they enhance student learning.

The effective use of films requires preparation and debriefing of the students to guide their learning. This advance work is frequently overlooked by faculty members and because of that the students often see no real purpose in watching films—other than for entertainment. Thus, the faculty member needs to ask, "What can I do to prepare the students so that they will get the most from this film?" and "What should I do when the film is over to ensure that they have grasped the main points?"

Slides are wonderful additions to many classes, but often faculty members do not consider that while the students are watching slides, they usually are not able to take notes because the room is dark. How can this limitation be overcome? In addition, the faculty member should ask, "How many slides should be shown during a single class session? Are slides the best medium for showing what we are studying or would videotape be better? Should I develop a set of controlled notes or handouts that help delineate the main points of the slide presentation?"

Examination of the overhead transparencies used by the faculty member can also provide some insight into the person's sense of humor, organization, understanding of why visuals are used, and so forth. Overheads copied directly from the text or made from typewritten material are more numerous than we would like to think. In addition, a large number of faculty members seem to think that the lights must be dimmed in order for students to see the overheads. While turning the lights down may be necessary in some rooms, it is often a big surprise to faculty that overhead projectors were developed primarily to enable the speaker to face the audience while talking rather than be constantly turning around to write on the blackboard. If the lights are dimmed, eye contact becomes nonexistent.

Handouts may be used to enhance what is discussed in class or to provide a way for the faculty member to communicate detailed concepts more effectively. They are especially useful for detailed illustrations, supplemental readings, and controlled notes. (Controlled notes provide a framework for student notetaking and usually include drawings and key terms. In order to understand these notes, however, the student must come to class and fill in the missing information.)

Ideally, the consultant will look at all of the course materials prior to attending the first class and assist the faculty members in digging into the whys and wherefores of their course planning. (In reality, however, consultants are often requested to attend the class first and analyze the various components later.)

Phase 3: Gather Information

Although some types of information are gathered in phase 2, the primary source of this information is the faculty member. In contrast, the information gathered in phase 3 is typically obtained from "others"—students, colleagues, observers, and the consultant. This information helps faculty members get a broader perspective on how their teaching affects students and how it is perceived by others who observe the teaching process. It is in this third phase that the consultant needs to have a broad repertoire of techniques and methods for gathering data and helping the faculty member interpret them. Some of the methods and instruments by which this information can be gathered, along with why the data might be useful, are listed below.

Student Evaluations from Previous Semesters/Quarters. Although this kind of data is covered in depth by Theall and Franklin (see Chapter Six), I call attention here to techniques used by consultants to help faculty members see trends and locate the good, along with the bad, in students' comments. The task of sifting through the numerous written comments of student evaluations often seems too laborious and not worth the effort to faculty members. Frequently, the only responses that "jump" out at them are those that contain negative criticism. However, because student evaluation data can often encourage a faculty member to make changes and seek assistance in doing so, a thorough analysis of the data can provide valuable information that might otherwise be overlooked.

Graphs of numerical averages for the same class over several years can readily reveal increases or decreases in student ratings of the course as a whole as well as specific aspects delineated by the various items on the evaluation forms. Even when numerical averages are charted, it is sometimes difficult to really appreciate how much they change over time. However, a bar graph quickly shows the level of each item over time as well as the relationship of each item to all of the other items.

Clustering of items that relate to the same types of teacher behaviors or teaching methods can also provide insight into possible deficiencies in need of correction. For example, on many evaluation forms there are a number of items that focus on the way that the instructor and students interrelate, that is, their rapport. By placing the numerical averages of each of these items next to one another or in a column, the consultant can probably determine what can be done to improve rapport. Perhaps the instructor was given high marks for "seemed sensitive to the feelings and needs of students" but at the same time received lower marks for "usually seemed to be aware of whether the class was following the presentation with understanding." Although, initially, these ratings may seem to negate each other, it might be that the faculty member really relates well to students before and after class and during office hours, but during the lectures he or she rarely asks for student responses to questions, seldom recognizes students who raise their hands, and does not leave time for anyone to respond when asked a question. Clustering of all of the low items and all of the high items can also be revealing. Frequently, the low items deal with relationships with students and the high items deal with knowledge of the content. An experienced consultant can provide these types of insights and help the faculty member see how the various items are or might be related to each other.

Use of a "written comments analysis grid" (Povlacs, 1984; Lewis, 1989) can alter faculty attitudes such as "All of the students say I'm unorganized" or "Only the students who don't like me or the course are saying I'm not responsive to student needs." The benefit of this grid technique is that it helps us find out whether students who highly rate a course are saying the same things as those who rate the course lower. For example, students who give the course an overall rating of 2 (low) may mention that more organization would be helpful. This is a comment that we might expect from someone who was not happy with the course. However, we can see that lack of organization can also be a concern for students who give the course an overall rating of 4 (high). To find out exactly what the students mean by "lack of organization," the faculty member can follow up by asking the students to identify (either in writing or verbally) specific instances in which it would have helped to have more organization.

Student Evaluations for Midsemester Feedback. When student ratings and other information are gathered for teaching improvement, data are usually collected near the midpoint of the term, since students will have had sufficient time to be able to evaluate the teacher's performance and the teacher will have had enough time to consider and perhaps even implement changes. Generally, such changes can be made if a problem is straightforward, for example, if the teacher does not give students enough time to take notes during lectures; but if the problem is more complex, it may not be correctible by the end of the term. Faculty have often been disappointed with their end-of-term evaluations because their ratings are not higher than those given at midterm. For this reason, teaching consultants should be careful not to raise hopes for improvement beyond reason. Nevertheless, a great deal of useful information can be gleaned from midterm evaluations. The following paragraphs describe some techniques for gathering midterm evaluation data.

Written Midsemester Feedback. Any written student evaluation form can be modified to obtain midsemester feedback from the students. With some additional modifications, the forms can be used to compare faculty members' responses to those of their students. The discrepancies between what the faculty members say and what the students say can serve to pinpoint areas in teaching method or communication style that need to be altered. One form that is already set up for this process is Teaching Analysis by Students (TABS) Form B (Bergquist and Phillips, 1975; Erickson and Erickson, 1979; Povlacs, 1988). This form of TABS has only twenty-five items and can be filled out quite rapidly. All of the items are Likert-scaled or multiple-choice items except for the final entry, which is an open-ended question.

One item that frequently reflects differences between faculty and student responses is "Making clear the distinction between major and minor topics." Often, faculty members do not cue their students about when an important topic is being discussed. Thus, the students get the impression that everything is important and that they must learn all of the material presented. If this item shows that what students think is quite different from what their instructor thinks, the consultant might brainstorm with the faculty member about possible ways to emphasize important points and concepts during the lecture. For example, the faculty member might list them on the board or overhead, move to a particular spot (such as behind the podium) prior to saying something important, and change his or her tone of voice.

Verbal Midsemester Feedback: Small Group Instructional Diagnosis (SGID). This method of acquiring student feedback has been shown to open the lines of communication between faculty and students (Clark and Beckey, 1979). SGID may be done in a number of ways, but the most common involves dividing the class into small groups of four to five students. The instructor leaves the room and the consultant lists three questions that the students should discuss. These usually are the following: (1) "What in the course has helped your learning the most or do you like the best?" (2) "What in the course has hindered your learning?" (3) "If you were the instructor, what changes would you make to avoid the problems mentioned in response to question 2?"

The students then appoint a secretary and spokesperson for each group and spend five to ten minutes discussing the three questions. At the conclusion of this time, the spokesperson for each group provides one of their answers to question 1. After each group has had a chance to list their answers to question 1, the groups report their answers to question 2, and so forth. The group responses may be written either on an overhead transparency or on the board so everyone can see them. (Use of an overhead transparency makes it easy for the consultant to take the answers back to the office to write the report for the faculty member. If responses are written on the board, the consultant should probably ask for a volunteer to write them on a piece of paper so as to secure a copy.) The most important aspect of this format is that the responses to questions 2 and 3 are paired: sources of problems and suggested solutions. In my written reports I usually put student suggestions in roman type and my suggestions in italics. Although the information obtained through this method may not be vastly different from that obtained on a written student evaluation (Tiberius, 1988), SGID seems to help students and faculty members become much more aware of each other as "real people," and some of the communication barriers are lifted.

Kolb Learning Styles Inventory (LSI) and Similar Inventories. Experience shows that most faculty members assume that they and their students learn and process information in exactly the same way. By discussing learning style differences and having students and faculty fill out the LSI (Kolb, 1984), we can collect hard data that demonstrate to faculty members the variety of learning styles among students in their courses. The four student learning styles identified in the LSI are briefly described below.

Divergers prefer to work with direct, concrete situations, viewing them from a variety of standpoints. These people have a diversity of ideas and are very adept at brainstorming and other creative endeavors. Also, they often enjoy working with others. Academic disciplines with members who often fall into this quadrant are the humanities and social and behavioral sciences.

Assimilators excel in the design of models to explain phenomena. Their talent is consolidation of observations into coherent systems, although they are not interested in the practical application of the theories that are developed. Academic disciplines with members in this quadrant are the basic sciences and math.

Convergers enjoy building logical systems that can be applied to real problems. This enjoyment does not mean that they wish to conduct the applications, but they do try to develop solutions to questions by logical analysis rather than by trial and error. An academic discipline with many convergers is engineering. This style is also quite common among university faculty.

Accommodators get the job done. They are not interested in why things operate the way that they do, as long as real problems are solved. If a theory does not work, these people discard it in favor of something more practical. They are willing to take risks and experiment until a solution is found. Learners with this type of preference are likely to be found in the applications fields such as education and business.

Sometimes I have found, especially in courses for nonmajors, that the faculty member's learning style is completely different from the styles of the students taking that course. It is no wonder, for example, that the instructor with a divergent learning style has difficulty communicating well with students who are assimilators, convergers, or accommodators. The information obtained through the LSI can be used by the consultant to encourage faculty members to incorporate a variety of teaching methods into their repertoires (Kolb, 1984; Svinicki and Dixon, 1987; Tobias, 1990).

The LSI is also an excellent means for assisting faculty members in the use of groups and group work in their classes. To ensure that a group is as productive as possible, as many of the LSI types as possible should be included. For example, if all of the people in group X are divergers, they may have a wealth of ideas about solving a given problem, but they may not be able to implement any of the proposed solutions. If, however, that group also includes an accommodator, the likelihood of something actually being accomplished increases dramatically.

Minute Papers. For most faculty members, the only time that they acquire feedback about their students' understanding of course content is when they give quizzes or exams. By asking students to write down the most important things learned during the current lecture, or during the previous lecture, a faculty member can obtain valuable information about how to prepare for the next class session (Wilson, 1984).

In-Class Observations. These observations can be made by a colleague or trained observer and provide several different types of data. One kind of data, a fairly subjective form, consists of notes taken during the class. Another kind of data, using an objective observation system, provides a more detailed and quantitative look at what is happening.

Subjective Observational Data. Notes taken during in-class observations can show whether or not the content of the class is organized in a logical manner, how easy or difficult it is to take coherent notes from the lecture, whether or not the faculty member clearly indicates the most important points, and how easy or difficult it is to read what is written on the board or on the overhead. In addition, comments about student participation, media used, voice projection, interactions with the students, and so forth can provide insights into what happened. Often, when faculty members look over notes of this kind, they see what they missed or realize that they did not clearly explain a topic. Caution is needed here, however: Consultants typically are very good note takers, and faculty members should be encouraged to look at the notes taken by students to get a more realistic picture of what the students thought was emphasized.

Objective Observational Data. Information about the interactions that occur in a class can be recorded using an objective observation system such as the Cognitive Interaction Analysis System (Flanders, 1970; Lewis, 1988; Lewis and Johnson, 1989). This kind of data can provide more detailed information about a number of aspects of the class session, including the cognitive level of questions that the instructor asks, the amount of student input and number of student questions that are allowed, the use of "wait time" after questions, the use of examples and analogies in the lecture, the length of time spent on a topic, and the amount of time spent answering student questions.

Objective observation data are very appealing to faculty members who are trained in research techniques. For example, they can be shown that they waited less than three seconds after asking a question. Then, after some practice, they can see that they are now waiting at least six seconds and that the answers provided by students are at a higher cognitive level than those provided in the past. It is very easy to "show" that change has occurred, and this improvement is positive reinforcement.

A Matrix of Data Needs and Sources

To provide some structure to the above information, Table 5.1 shows how one might decide which data sources to use to gather information about various aspects of the instructional process. Across the top of the matrix are listed the three main areas about which a consultant may wish to obtain data: course information, instructor information, and student information. These areas are then divided into more specific topic areas. Down the left-hand side of the matrix are listed sources of information or data. These have been clustered into three areas: written data sources, oral data sources, and audiovisual data sources.

The check marks indicate which data sources might be most appropriate for obtaining information about a certain area. For example, if a consultant wished to find out how a course is organized, a copy of the syllabus would be useful. Additional sources of data on course organization can be found in the objectives and goals for the course, the textbooks, homework and assignments, notes from in-class observations, comments from student evaluations, and so forth. Depending on the concerns of the faculty member, the consultant will find some sources more informative and appropriate than others. Moreover, the consultant does not have to obtain data from all of the sources that have been checked.

Using Teaching Improvement Data

Chapters One, Two, and Three of this volume provide important details about effective teacher-consultant interactions. We can apply those chapters to just about any feedback context; we need only remember the importance of keeping the client involved and active in the process. Below, I provide brief guidelines on presenting feedback data to faculty for teaching improvement.

Some of the most common means of data presentation are in written form (which may include lists that summarize the data and present recommendations), oral form (including discussions after class), and graphical form (which presents changes over time). Whichever method is used to present findings, it is important to (1) present positive aspects first and then move on to those areas that need improvement, (2) focus on only two or

Table 5.1. Matrix of Data Needs and Sources

Information needed about: Source of Information/Data	Course Information					Instructor Information			Student Information	
	Subject Matter	Course Organization	Physical Facilities	Evaluation Process	Change Over Time	Teaching Skills	Rapport	Time Constraints	Student Experiences	Student Learning
Written Data Sources										
Course Catalogues	✓								✓	
Course Schedule			✓					✓[a]	✓[b]	
Other College/Univ. Documents	✓							✓[c]		
Syllabus	✓	✓	✓	✓	✓			✓	✓	✓
Objectives/Goals	✓	✓		✓	✓	✓			✓	✓
Textbooks	✓	✓								
Readings	✓								✓	✓
Homework/Assignments	✓	✓		✓	✓	✓	✓		✓	✓
Exams	✓									
Grade Distributions	✓			✓	✓	✓				✓
Minute Papers	✓			✓		✓				✓
In-class Observation Notes	✓	✓			✓	✓	✓		✓	✓
Obj. Obs. System		✓			✓	✓	✓		✓	
Student Written Eval.										
Numeric					✓	✓	✓			
Graphed	✓			✓	✓	✓	✓		✓	
Item Clusters	✓	✓		✓	✓	✓	✓		✓	

Written Comments	✓	✓	✓	✓	✓	✓	✓		✓	✓
Analysis Grid									✓	
Background Info Sheets										
Learning Styles Inventory		✓								
Check-Lists	✓		✓		✓	✓	✓	✓		
Rating Scales			✓		✓	✓	✓		✓	
Oral Data Sources										
Initial Interview	✓	✓	✓		✓	✓	✓		✓	
Small Group Instructional Diagnosis (SGID)	✓	✓	✓			✓	✓			✓
Oral Presentations-students										✓
Questioning by Instructor							✓		✓	✓
Visual/Aural Data Sources										
AV aids Films	✓		✓			✓	✓		✓	
Slides	✓	✓	✓			✓	✓		✓	
Transparencies	✓	✓	✓			✓	✓		✓	
AV equipment available			✓					✓	✓	
Seating Arrangement			✓			✓	✓			
Accoustics			✓			✓	✓		✓	
Videotape of Instructor	✓	✓	✓		✓		✓		✓	

[a] To find out what other classes the faculty member is teaching
[b] To find out any prerequisite courses
[c] To find out what other committees faculty member is on

three things to improve at any one time, (3) make at least one of the features to improve very achievable and measurable, if possible, (4) encourage the faculty member to suggest ways to achieve the desired changes, (5) include written explanations of any specialized data-gathering techniques used so that the faculty member will be able to analyze and understand the suggestions at a later time, and (6) follow up after the faculty member has had some time to work on the skills and methods.

In many faculty/instructional development centers, the data gathered during the individual consultation process are confidential. This means that only the faculty member will be given copies of the data and any explanations of data interpretation. The faculty member, however, is free to make copies of the data and reports to submit to administrators or to share with colleagues.

Ensuring Follow-up. At the conclusion of an individual consultation process, the faculty member and consultant may decide to meet again at a later date for several follow-up sessions. These may include in-class observations, self-reports, midsemester evaluations conducted for several semesters and summarized by the consultant, and so forth. Follow-up should be an integral part of this process to ensure that the faculty member does not slip back into old habits once the short-term formal consultation process is completed.

For example, I worked with one faculty member who had her classes videotaped at least once a year for four years after we had completed the intensive part of the consultation process. After each videotape was made, we then sat down, reviewed her goals and objectives, viewed the videotape, and noted any new concerns or problems that had surfaced. After the fourth time of following these steps, we both decided that she was maintaining her newly acquired skills and techniques and that she was now able to recognize problems herself and come up with ways to solve them.

Leading Faculty Toward Self-Diagnosis. One of the main goals of individual consultation is very similar to that of teaching: the learner's, or faculty member's, self-sufficiency and self-motivation. When faculty members understand the process, they then become life-long learners, and the ability to monitor changes in teaching and learning becomes a part of their lives. Of course, consultants will always be available to provide encouragement and support, but the faculty members should now have the framework and tools to recognize problem areas and come up with ways to change.

References

Aleamoni, L. M. "The Usefulness of Student Evaluations in Improving College Teaching." *Instructional Science,* 1978, 7 (1), 95–105.

Bergquist, W. H., and Phillips, S. R. *A Handbook for Faculty Development.* Vol. 1. Washington, D.C.: Council for the Advancement of Small Colleges, 1975.

Centra, J. A. "Formative and Summative Evaluation: Parody or Paradox?" In L. M. Aleamoni (ed.), *Techniques for Evaluating and Improving Instruction.* New Directions for Teaching and Learning, no. 31. San Francisco: Jossey-Bass, 1987.

Clark, J., and Beckey, J. "Use of Small Groups in Instructional Evaluation." *POD Quarterly,* 1979, *1,* 87-95.

Cohen, P. A. "Effectiveness of Student-Rating Feedback for Improving College Instruction: A Meta-Analysis of Findings." *Research in Higher Education,* 1980, *13* (4), 321-341.

Coil, A., and Bean, T. "Text Structure and Critical Reading." *Journal of College Reading and Learning,* 1980, *13,* 98-102.

Erickson, G. R., and Erickson, B. L. "Improving College Teaching: An Evaluation of a Teaching Consultation Procedure." *Journal of Higher Education,* 1979, *50,* 670-683.

Flanders, N. A. *Analyzing Teaching Behavior.* Reading, Mass.: Addison-Wesley, 1970.

Kolb, D. A. *Experiential Learning: Experience as the Source of Learning and Development.* Englewood Cliffs, N.J.: Prentice Hall, 1984.

Lewis, K. G. *The Large Class Analysis Project.* Final report. Austin: Center for Teaching Effectiveness, University of Texas, 1982. (ED 260 089)

Lewis, K. G. "Using an Objective Observation System to Diagnose Teaching Problems." In K. G. Lewis (ed.), *Face to Face: A Sourcebook of Individual Consultation Techniques for Faculty/Instructional Developers.* Stillwater, Okla.: New Forums Press, 1988.

Lewis, K. G. "Making Sense (and Use) of Written Student Evaluation Comments." *Center for Teaching Effectiveness Newsletter,* 1989, *10* (4), 1-2.

Lewis, K. G., and Johnson, G. R. *Monitoring Your Classroom Communication Skills: A Programmed Workbook for Developing Coding Skills Using Johnson's Cognitive Interaction Analysis System (CIAS) and Expanded CIAS.* Austin: Center for Teaching Effectiveness, University of Texas, 1989.

McKeachie, W. J. "Can Evaluating Instruction Improve Teaching?" In L. M. Aleamoni (ed.), *Techniques for Evaluating and Improving Instruction.* New Directions for Teaching and Learning, no. 31. San Francisco: Jossey-Bass, 1987.

Menges, R. J. "Using Evaluative Information to Improve Instruction." In P. Seldin and Associates (eds.), *How Administrators Can Improve Teaching: Moving from Talk to Action in Higher Education.* San Francisco: Jossey-Bass, 1990.

Povlacs, J. T. "Reading Students' Written Comments on Evaluations of Teaching." In L. Buhl and L. Wilson (eds.), *To Improve the Academy: Resources for Student, Faculty, and Institutional Development.* Vol. 3. Stillwater, Okla.: POD and New Forums Press, 1984.

Povlacs, J. T. "The Teaching Analysis Program and the Role of the Consultant." In K. G. Lewis (ed.), *Face to Face: A Sourcebook of Individual Consultation Techniques for Faculty/Instructional Developers.* Stillwater, Okla.: New Forums Press, 1988.

Svinicki, M. D., and Dixon, N. M. "The Kolb Model Modified for Classroom Activities." *College Teaching,* 1987, *35* (4), 141-146.

Taylor-Way, D. "Consultation with Video: Memory Management Through Stimulated Recall." In K. G. Lewis (ed.), *Face to Face: A Sourcebook of Individual Consultation Techniques for Faculty/Instructional Developers.* Stillwater, Okla.: New Forums Press, 1988.

Tiberius, R. G. "The Use of the Discussion Group for the Fine Tuning of Teaching." In K. G. Lewis (ed.), *Face to Face: A Sourcebook of Individual Consultation Techniques for Faculty/Instructional Developers.* Stillwater, Okla.: New Forums Press, 1988.

Tobias, S. *They're Not Dumb, They're Different: Stalking the Second Tier.* Tucson, Ariz.: Research Corporation—A Foundation for the Advancement of Science, 1990.

Weimer, M. *Improving College Teaching: Strategies for Developing Instructional Effectiveness.* San Francisco: Jossey-Bass, 1990.

Weimer, M., Parrett, J. L., and Kerns, M. *How Am I Teaching?: Forms and Activities for Acquiring Instructional Input.* Madison, Wis.: Magna, 1988.

Wilson, R. *Using Consultation to Improve Teaching.* Technical report. Berkeley: Teaching and Evaluation Service, University of California, 1984. (ED 242 271)

Karron G. Lewis is assistant director of the Center for Teaching Effectiveness at the University of Texas, Austin.

In a student rating report, a mean may have little meaning in the absence of reliable, valid data and appropriate bases for comparing it to some standard. To use ratings results effectively and accurately, guidelines for understanding data are critical. Why, then, are they so often absent?

Using Student Ratings for Teaching Improvement

Michael Theall, Jennifer Franklin

As many contributors to this volume point out, the most effective kind of feedback for teaching improvement combines valid and concrete information with the assistance of a knowledgeable person in a nonthreatening environment. Also acknowledged by writers and practitioners in evaluation and teaching improvement is the fact that student ratings of instruction are the most available and most commonly used source of feedback for both teaching improvement and personnel decision making (Seldin, 1989). Unfortunately, student ratings are also the kind of data most frequently misinterpreted and misused by faculty and administrators (Franklin and Theall, 1989). However, this finding is tempered by the fact that the same research also found that instructional specialists and teaching improvement practitioners (some of whom were also faculty) had significantly higher levels of knowledge about evaluation practice and the use and interpretation of student ratings than did faculty colleagues who were not involved in teaching improvement activities. Nonetheless, the tasks of interpreting and using ratings are not simple and are often confounded by the various levels of complexity imposed by the contexts in which they are used (Theall and Franklin, 1990).

In Chapter Four of this volume, Peter Gray offers an approach to gathering and using data for teaching improvement. In Chapter Five, Karron Lewis considers various sources of data, including student input from small group instructional diagnosis. The purpose of this chapter is to provide guidelines for using student ratings for teaching improvement, with special attention given to the teaching consultation process.

We begin by grounding the process of teaching improvement consultation in the theoretical context of dimensions and specific behaviors associated with effective teaching. We do this to give the practitioner and faculty client common ground for evaluating teaching performance. When consultation is understood as a learning process (for both client and consultant), this framework makes instructional sense as well. We concentrate primarily on the following issues: the dimensions and behaviors of teaching that can be evaluated using ratings, useful questions to include in the evaluation effort, technical characteristics of valid and reliable questionnaires and items, use of student comments, useful analyses and reports, interpretation of results, and "other issues" for the consultant who uses ratings feedback.

The Dimensions and Behaviors of Teaching

There has been considerable investigation of the dimensionality of teaching. Conclusions have been generally similar, identifying teaching (and its evaluation) as multidimensional (Cohen, 1981; Feldman, 1976; Marsh, 1987) and specifying the dimensions as similar. Recently, Abrami and d'Apollonia (1990) identified twenty-four dimensions: (1) stimulation of interest, (2) enthusiasm, (3) knowledge of the subject, (4) intellectual expansiveness, (5) preparation and organization, (6) clarity and understandableness, (7) elocutionary skills, (8) class level and progress, (9) clarity of course objectives, (10) relevance and value of course material, (11) relevance and usefulness of supplementary materials, (12) workload, (13) perceived outcome, (14) fairness of evaluation, (15) classroom management, (16) personality characteristics, (17) feedback, (18) encouragement of discussion and diversity of opinion, (19) intellectual challenge and encouragement of independent thought, (20) concern and respect for students, (21) availability and helpfulness, (22) overall course, (23) overall instructor, and (24) miscellaneous items.

Many of these dimensions are not appropriate for use in personnel decisions, but each dimension is potentially important for teaching improvement. While some dimensions are general (for example, 22 and 23), others are more specific and can be investigated in detail. An overall rating of teaching performance (23), although summary in nature, is not necessarily the "average" of more specific ratings. In fact, ratings on specific teaching skill areas may be very different from overall ratings. The teaching consultant can help faculty to identify areas or dimensions in need of attention and can also show how items that probe specific dimensions of teaching can relate to overall ratings.

An effective way to use student ratings to assess performance in each of the dimensions listed above is, as Murray (1983) has suggested, to approach teaching in terms of "low-inference" behaviors, that is, specific, unambiguous behaviors that can be isolated and observed without interference from the value system of the observer or other confounding factors. The benefit of this approach to teaching improvement is that when important teaching skills are assessed through low-inference behaviors, areas of weakness become identifiable and amenable to change. Low-inference behaviors can often be learned without difficulty. Thus, faculty can quickly gain skill in these behaviors.

As suggested elsewhere in this volume, the initial targets for teaching improvement should be those behaviors that can be clearly identified and addressed. Less likely for success are attempts to alter long-standing patterns of working or cognitive style, strongly held philosophical beliefs, orientations to one's field or toward teaching, and personality characteristics. In many instances, as George Geis suggests in Chapter One, it would be presumptuous to suggest changes in these areas based on the results of one evaluation.

Useful Items to Include in Ratings Questionnaires

If the goal is to determine whether behaviors associated with effective teaching occur and to measure how often, a ratings questionnaire must address those behaviors. Items that probe behaviors generally associated with effective teaching as well as items specific to content area instructional techniques (such as labs or case studies) give useful information when students agree in their responses.

However, students may disagree in their perceptions of what happens in a classroom. What is helpful for one student may not be effective for others. Proper use of ratings feedback in consultation requires an understanding of the sources of disagreement as well as the common ground. Instruction is not a unilateral process. Students should be active participants in the teaching-learning process. Many characteristics of students, such as their backgrounds, prior preparation, general attitudes toward the content area of the course, achievement level (grade point average [GPA]), and expected course grades, can be helpful in understanding responses to items that probe low-inference teaching behaviors. For example, students may disagree strongly in their responses to an item that probes whether the pace of instruction is appropriate for their skill levels. If the consultant can determine that students with low GPAs tended to be dissatisfied with the pace compared with those with middle to high GPAs, then the consultant has an important clue about what is happening in the course and how instruction can be improved for the low-GPA students.

It is also helpful to use two or three very general items that probe satisfaction with the course, teacher, and amount learned (Cashin and Downey, 1991). These items can help the consultant and faculty member form a more reliable general impression of students' feelings than can be achieved by averaging (unweighted) results from more specific, individual items.

Technical Considerations

Teaching improvement consultation requires ratings instruments that contain a combination of general and specific items probing aspects of instruction associated with effective teaching. The securing of such questionnaires and items is more problematic.

There are three ways to address the instrumentation problem. The first is to employ a questionnaire that has already been validated and extensively used (for example, the IDEA form developed at Kansas State University, the Teaching Analysis by Students form developed at the University of Massachusetts, the Teacher-Course Evaluation Project Questionnaire developed at Northeastern University, the Course/Instructor Evaluation Questionnaire from the University of Arizona, and the Student Evaluation of Educational Quality form developed at the University of California). The second is to develop and validate a questionnaire locally, although this is a difficult and time-consuming process (see Arreola and Aleamoni, 1990; Berk, 1979; Theall and Franklin, 1991). The third strategy is to tailor-make a questionnaire by selecting items from an item bank. In each case, the instrument constructed should contain items that allow clear interpretation, probe only one issue at a time, and state the issue in unambiguous terms. As suggested above, low-inference items are useful for examining teaching skills. For example, in dealing with the dimension of clarity, Murray (1983) suggests questionnaire items that investigate the following teaching activities: (1) providing frequent examples, (2) defining new or unfamiliar terms, (3) repeating difficult ideas, (4) using graphs or diagrams, (5) pointing out practical applications, (6) suggesting ways to memorize, (7) writing key terms on the board or overhead screen, and (8) answering questions thoroughly.

The strategy of local development of questionnaires should remain a major area for concern. For while the temptation to locally develop such forms is great, the end result is often invalid and unreliable data, especially when faculty develop the forms without expert assistance. In a study of the evaluation items chosen by faculty, Ory and Wieties (1991) reported that the ten items most frequently chosen from a cafeteria-style item bank included questions about instructor preparedness (ranked first), instructor knowledge (third), grading practices (fourth), and enjoyment of teaching (eighth). From a utilitarian viewpoint, these are items of dubious value, and, in fact, items on preparedness and knowledge are generally considered invalid because students, at best, can only report their own impressions of an instructor's apparent subject expertise. Presumably, a subject matter expert would be better qualified to rate preparation and knowledge. Only two of the frequently chosen items in Ory and Wieties's study approached low inference: "How well did exam questions reflect content and emphasis of the course?" (fifth) and "The instructor stated clearly what was expected of students" (sixth). Thus, faculty item choices not only appeared to yield less information about specific teaching behaviors than is needed for teaching improvement purposes but at the same time provided other information of questionable value.

Wording of Items and Response Options

The wording of items and response options should be clear and consistent. A good combination includes questions phrased as statements of behavior and either a frequency or an agree-disagree response scale. For example, the question stem might state, "The instructor presented information at a rate I could follow." Note the use of the personal pronoun "I" rather than the less precise word "students." Individuals do not always know the feelings of other students and therefore questions should not ask them to estimate the opinions of others. With either the frequency or the agreement scale, this item can provide a clear picture of the effectiveness of the instructor's pacing for each student and, by inference, for the group, because most students are likely to understand the question in the same way. But if the item were phrased, "The instructor paced the instruction appropriately" or "The instructor presented information at an appropriate pace," variation in students' definitions of "appropriate pace" would make interpretation more difficult. Moreover, if the item read, "Rate the appropriateness of the instructor's pacing," and the response scale covered five points from "excellent" through "average" to "poor," two definitions come into play: one for "appropriateness" and a second for the response adjective chosen. Clearly, this item is likely to be even less reliable than the previous example.

The preceding discussion illustrates how item construction can affect the overall usefulness of a questionnaire. The need for reliable information argues for the use of a validated instrument or the consultation of measurement and evaluation experts. If an instrument is locally developed, then careful field tests, analysis, and validation are always required.

Student Comments

Almost all student rating systems allow the inclusion of written comments. Most faculty pay close attention to these comments, and some administrators want to see them for use in promotion and tenure decisions. Narrative comments are given great weight. Our experience has been that about 10 percent of a class responds with narrative comments unless an extreme situation arises, whether good or bad. In the extreme cases, comments match quantitative results in terms of frequency and intensity, but in more "normal" situations (that is, "average" ratings in courses with normal distributions of scores) comments usually come from either the very satisfied or the very dissatisfied. It is easy to overinterpret these comments. It is also dangerous because they represent so small a percentage of the class. If we are unwilling to accept quantitative data from fewer than half the students, (the minimal standard described in Table 6.1), we should not be willing to make decisions based on a 10 percent sample simply because the information is in written rather than numerical form.

This minimal standard of 50 percent does not mean that student comments are unusable for teaching improvement. Indeed, student comments can provide very valuable insights into classroom processes and activities or into teacher behavior. But they should guide further investigation and be used in conjunction with other kinds of data, rather than solely to determine a course of action or a decision. Articulate, insightful student comments can be a potent tool for illustrating what quantitative data show in more abstract terms.

Analyses and Reports

At minimum, analysis of evaluation results for teaching improvement should include descriptive information (distributions of responses by item), measures of central tendency (mean, median, standard deviation), and a direct estimate of error such as confidence intervals for means. Although global items, factorially derived, or other composite scores for subsets of items that probe several aspects of a single topic are often recommended for personnel decision-making purposes, they are probably less useful for providing feedback for teaching improvement unless accompanied by more specific information.

While the purpose of teaching improvement evaluation is not to compare the performance of individuals, interpretation of results is clearer if performance can be measured against some standard. Centra (1979) has suggested that comparisons made among faculty can help motivate poor performers to improve. Certainly, comparisons among course offerings over time for a single teacher can demonstrate the effects of efforts to improve. Analyses comparing individual results to some norm usually involve t-values or other standardized scores, or percentile-ranked means with confidence intervals, and they require a sufficiently large data base of course evaluations. Generally, teaching improvement purposes do not require that individuals be so rigorously compared to standards derived from some group or even from their own past performances.

For comparisons among teachers, the most logical standards are the norms for the group (course, department, college, institution, or national data base). But recent research has emphasized the importance of avoiding comparative judgments when the bases for comparison are ill-defined. Cashin (1990) has shown consistent differences in ratings as a function of disciplinary differences, and Franklin and Theall (1991) report large and significant negative effects of class size on both student ratings and student performance. While these findings argue, once again, for caution in the interpretation of results, they do not mean that interpretation is impossible. Good reports, useful guides, and knowledgeable assistance are required for this purpose.

Interpreting Reports

When reports are produced, they should present information clearly and should be accompanied by guides for interpretation and use. All too often, evaluations are processed (by default) in a campus computer center and the only feedback received by faculty is a set of numbers on "green bar" computer paper.

Steps can be taken by individuals and practitioners to help ensure valid interpretation of data. First, examine the size of the class, the number of students responding, and the ratio of these figures. Table 6.1 presents a general set of guidelines.

Second, examine each item to determine the percentage of omitted responses. Even in a good sample, some items may have been left blank because they did not apply or because students were unsure of their responses. Reduce the response ratio for the item by the percentage of blank or omitted responses and reconsider its usefulness.

Third, review the distributions of responses and the mean scores and standard deviations of individual items. Some reports of results provide this information for all items regardless of whether the information is meaningful. For example, "workload" and "difficulty" are often misinterpreted because some value is attached to heavy workload or extreme course difficulty under the automatic assumption that "heavy and hard" results in poor ratings or that "light workload" and "easier" levels of difficulty signal poor teaching. These statements have no stronger empirical basis than does the argument that good ratings can be "bought" with high grades or that teachers who are "easy" receive higher ratings. Franklin and Theall (1991) have shown that there is a significant and positive relationship between challenge and ratings. Students gave higher ratings and demon-

Table 6.1. Sample Size and Response Ratio Standards for Student Rating Data

Class Size (N)	Minimum Acceptable Response Ratio
5–20	80 percent
21–30	75 percent
30–50	66 percent[a]
50–100	50 percent[b]
> 100	50 percent

[a] 75 percent recommended

[b] 66 percent recommended

strated higher levels of achievement in courses that were rated as "more difficult" because they had achieved more. They also gave high ratings to courses and instructors when courses were less difficult as long as they felt that they had learned something. And in the several thousand courses in the sample, there was no evidence whatever to support the "grade inflation" hypothesis. If there were attempts to "buy" higher ratings with higher grades, students were having no part of it.

The mean is the arithmetic average of student responses for an item. Means for ratings items often range from 1 to 5. Check the response options on the evaluation form used to be certain of correct interpretation. One characteristic of student ratings that has been reliably observed during the last several decades of teacher-course evaluation is the tendency of students to rate instructors favorably. Thus, the "average instructor" is typically rated around 3.5. This produces a skew toward the high end of the scale, and the otherwise bell-shaped curve of instructor ratings becomes "asymmetric."

The standard deviation for individual items is an index of agreement or disagreement among student raters. Perfect agreement yields a standard deviation of 0. Deviations of less than 1.0 indicate relatively good agreement in a 5-point scale.

Deviations of 1.2 and higher indicate that the mean may not be a good measure of student agreement. This situation may occur when opinion in a class is strongly divided between very high and very low ratings or, possibly, is evenly dispersed across the entire response scale, resulting in a mean that does not represent a "typical" student opinion in any meaningful sense. Because students vary in their needs, just as teachers vary in their skills, a teacher may be "among the best" for some and at the same time "among the worst" for others. A mean of 3.0 or 3.5 cannot be construed to represent "average" performance in the sense of middle-range performance when the mean is simply an artifact of strong disagreement among students. The standard deviation is therefore an important source of information about student opinion.

While means with small deviations can be understood to represent student opinion in the semantic sense (for example, "there was good agreement among students that this course was among the best they had taken"), means alone are not recommended for comparisons among courses. The majority of means fall within one standard deviation above or below the grand mean (the "mean of means"), and few people score extremely high or low. To make distinctions between scores in the midrange between very high and very low means is to risk overinterpreting chance differences in scores. For personnel decision making, use *t*-scores, percentile-ranked groups, or other appropriate measures of relative performance. In teaching improvement, use means only to locate the individual's performance in context. Obviously, improvement efforts are not necessary if an individual is performing well with respect to the norms for the department or school, barring the unlikely situation that the unit norms are themselves depressed. In such a case, improvement efforts on a larger scale may be warranted.

When Good Teaching Is "Average"

As noted earlier, one characteristic of student ratings that has been reliably observed during the last several decades of teacher-course evaluation is the tendency of students to rate instructors favorably. Thus, mean scores that are equivalent to "about average" in the original response scale may be grouped among the lower middle in percentile-ranked groups or may be distant from the mean in a t or other standardized score.

In effect, any score in a sample group in which no instructor was rated less than "better than average" is not a poor or even a mediocre score, even if its percentile group equivalent is low. Here is a concrete example: All faculty in a department receive overall ratings of 4.0 or higher (5.0 is the best possible rating). The norms on this item for the school and the institution are 3.7 and 3.5, respectively, so Instructor X (whose rating is 4.2) is considered, in the language of the item, "better than most instructors I have had." But Instructor X falls in the seventeenth percentile of the department, a ranking that carries a very different meaning from what the student raters intended. If the range of scores is very small, percentile rankings ranging from top to bottom represent trivial differences in mean score equivalents. In such circumstances comparison of ratings is not an appropriate method for making distinctions among instructors. Other sources of data are essential.

Other Considerations

Although more than three decades of research have shown student ratings to be quite dependable, there are a few predictable sources of systematic variation that should always be considered in comparing scores. For example, here are a few conclusions from the research (see Arreola and Aleamoni, 1990; Cashin, 1990; Centra, 1979; Franklin and Theall, 1991; Marsh, 1987): (1) Students tend to rank instructors teaching small classes (less than ten or fifteen) most highly, followed by those with sixteen to thirty-five students and those with over one hundred. Thus, the least favorably rated are classes with thirty-five to one hundred students. (2) Students tend to give slightly higher ratings to their majors or electives than to courses taken to fulfill a college requirement. (3) Courses in the humanities tend to be rated more highly than those in the physical sciences. (4) Student ratings can be biased by failure to adhere to instructions for administering a questionnaire. For example, failure of the instructor to leave the room during administration, failure to preserve student anonymity, administering of the evaluation during finals, and use of prejudicial introductory remarks can invalidate ratings results. (5) Time of day and scheduling factors appear to have little or no influence on ratings. (However, there may be systematic differences in who attends classes at particular times, which may have some impact on ratings.) (6) Academic ability of students as measured by GPA has shown little relationship to the ratings that they give. That is, "poor" students are just as appreciative of good teaching as are "good" students, while good students are just as critical of poor teaching as are less able students. And both types of student can easily tell the difference. (7) The practices of giving students unearned good grades and reducing the effort needed to earn grades have been demonstrated to have virtually no payoff of raising ratings in the long run, provided that ratings are anonymous.

Other Issues for Consultants

Knowledge of the literature on student ratings and of relevant issues of measurement and statistics is important for teaching consultants because helping faculty to interpret evaluation reports is one of the most common kinds of assistance that consultants provide. But there are other, equally important data-related issues for teaching consultants. The following sections outline some of these issues and explain why these kinds of information are valuable.

Establish Procedures to Document the Consultation Process and Its Results. For teaching improvement, documentation serves both the client and the consultant. For example, both consultant and client have a record for future reference, and the consultant can use the documentation to improve consultation skills.

Help the Institution to Use Ratings Accurately and Effectively. The teaching improvement consultant is often the only person available to provide information about the valid uses of ratings in the personnel decision-making process. Many faculty and administrators believe that where ratings forms are concerned, more is better, that is, more items provide a better basis for personnel decision making. However, ratings used for teaching improvement must first be confidential. The detail required for effective use of ratings in teaching improvement can be easily misinterpreted in the context of personnel decision making. The differences between contexts of application pose a particular problem for the consultant who is asked by a teacher to provide an administrative decision maker with copies of the results obtained with a diagnostic ratings form.

A standard diagnostic questionnaire might, for example, contain items about leading discussions. However, in a very large lecture class of one hundred or more students, it is very difficult to conduct useful in-class discussions regularly, if at all. If the response scale for the questionnaire ranges from "almost always" to "almost never," students might report that the instructor "rarely" or "almost never" conducted meaningful discussions. This item can be ignored by the instructor, who correctly views the responses as an artifact of the teaching situation. But if the report were made available to others unfamiliar with the class and they did not note the class size, then a serious interpretive error could result to the detriment of the instructor.

Be Aware of the Usefulness of Other Data. Just as specific questions can be useful for gaining an understanding of the behavior of the teacher, other data are important for understanding the students and the situation. Conclusions drawn about teaching in the absence of this information are reached with much more difficulty and are prone to more error; thus, teaching improvement evaluation should always consider these other sources of data. Knowledge about student motivation, prior preparation, class, and GPA, for example, can help the consultant understand why some students report that they cannot follow lectures or that they find tests extremely difficult.

Another important reason for collecting information about students is that it may prevent misinterpretation of results about faculty. In fact, for the protection of faculty, ratings items about students should also be considered in interpreting ratings results for personnel decisions. Consider the following case taken from actual data.

Professor Y requested help from a teaching consultant in interpreting recent student ratings. The consultant noted the following pertinent information about the teaching situation and its evaluation: (1) ratings were somewhat lower than usual on the overall items, (2) ratings were low on items relating to testing, pacing, relevance, and clarification of problems, (3) many items had unusually high standard deviations, and (4) the course's workload was considered "heavy" and the course was rated "more difficult than average." All in all, ratings were considerably lower than usual for this instructor and were marginal in comparison to the norms for the department. The overall ratings of the course were to appear in the ratings catalog and were probably going to be considered in an upcoming tenure decision. Professor Y was concerned about whether this evaluation would help or hinder a favorable decision. The consultant responded that the effect might depend on whether the results would be fully interpreted.

After reviewing the results, Professor Y and the consultant decided to inspect other information. A check of student demographics revealed the following: (1) About 40 percent of the class were seniors, 40 percent were freshmen, and the rest were equally divided among the other classes. (2) These percentages were similar to the distributions of responses on the items about prior preparation of students, difficulty, pacing, and, in fact, most of the specific items with depressed scores. Also, a review of teaching load revealed that since employment four years prior, this teacher had taught only upper-level or graduate courses. The conclusion (borne out by further analysis of the evaluation results) was that he succeeded with upper-level students, but the lower-level students had difficulty keeping up and thus were negative in their opinions.

Are the depressed ratings the teacher's "fault" alone or are they also related to a scheduling coincidence and a curriculum problem? One could make a case for the latter explanation and lessen the effect of this set of ratings on an overall assessment of the teacher's performance. As a result of the evaluation, some departmental changes might be made in the requirement for this course or its placement in the curriculum. Also, the teacher might decide (if possible) to focus on upper-level courses, or to work with a colleague who has been effective with beginning students, or to work with a teaching consultant to investigate the situation in more depth and to develop strategies for teaching lower-level students. Although this consultation began with the client's concern about the effect of ratings on tenure prospects, the information provided by the evaluation also created a starting point for improvements that could benefit the teacher, the students, and the institution.

When evaluations are used for promotion and tenure, the accepted rule is that no single evaluation should be considered adequate for decision making. In the above case, the instructor's overall record of good evaluations lessened the negative impact of one particular set of results. But in teaching improvement, consultants may be tempted to provide guidance based on a single set of results. Practitioners would do well to remember L'Hommedieu and Menges's (1990) caution about the quality of samples used in studies of ratings feedback. They reported that, in general, the conclusions of feedback studies were based on very small, often inadequate, samples and that generalizations arising from classroom studies should be carefully made. Likewise, teaching improvement practitioners would be well advised to avoid making generalizations about teaching performance based on the results of one application of a ratings instrument. Consultations based solely on a single sample of data should focus on understanding what happened in that particular class rather than attempt to characterize the teacher's typical performance. However, if the consultant has additional data from classroom observations, interviews with students, and other modes of evaluation, a single set of ratings may be useful for illustrative purposes. The important point is that decisions about useful strategies for improvement should not be based on a single sample of ratings data.

Summary

Teaching improvement efforts require valid and reliable information, which students can provide efficiently and effectively through the use of ratings questionnaires. In order for the data to be useful and for the processes of improvement to succeed, a series of careful steps must be followed. In particular, consultants and faculty need to know how different evaluative purposes affect evaluation results and they must be able to interpret and use the data at hand. Ill-informed decisions not only waste time and resources but also have negative effects on the faculty, the students, and the institution.

References

Abrami, P. C., and d'Apollonia, S. "The Dimensionality of Ratings and Their Use in Personnel Decisions." In M. Theall and J. Franklin (eds.), *Student Ratings of Instruction: Issues for Improving Practice.* New Directions for Teaching and Learning, no. 43. San Francisco: Jossey-Bass, 1990.

Arreola, R. A., and Aleamoni, L. M. "Practical Decisions in Developing and Operating a Faculty Evaluation System." In M. Theall and J. Franklin (eds.), *Student Ratings of Instruction: Issues for Improving Practice.* New Directions for Teaching and Learning, no. 43. San Francisco: Jossey-Bass, 1990.

Berk, R. A. "The Construction of Rating Instruments for Faculty Evaluation." *Journal of Higher Education,* 1979, 50, 650–669.

Cashin, W. E. "Students Do Rate Different Academic Fields Differently." In M. Theall and J. Franklin (eds.), *Student Ratings of Instruction: Issues for Improving Practice.* New Directions for Teaching and Learning, no. 43. San Francisco: Jossey-Bass, 1990.

Cashin, W. E., and Downey, R. G. "Using Global Student Ratings Items for Summative Evaluation." Paper presented at the 75th annual meetings of the American Educational Research Association, Chicago, April 1991.

Centra, J. A. *Determining Faculty Effectiveness: Assessing Teaching, Research, and Service for Personnel Decisions and Improvement.* San Francisco: Jossey-Bass, 1979.

Cohen, P. A. "Student Ratings of Instruction and Student Achievement: A Meta-Analysis of Multisection Validity Studies." *Review of Educational Research,* 1981, 51, 281–309.

Feldman, K. A. "The Superior College Teacher from the Students' View." *Research in Higher Education,* 1976, 5, 243–288.

Franklin, J., and Theall, M. "Who Reads Ratings: Knowledge, Attitudes, and Practices of Users of Student Ratings of Instruction." Paper presented at the 73rd annual meetings of the American Educational Research Association, San Francisco, April 1989.

Franklin, J., and Theall, M. "Grade Inflation and Student Ratings: A Closer Look." Paper presented at the 75th annual meetings of the American Educational Research Association, Chicago, April 1991.

L'Hommedieu, R. L., and Menges, R. J. "Toward More Conclusive Studies of Ratings Feedback." Paper presented at the 74th annual meetings of the American Educational Research Association, Boston, April 1990.

Marsh, H. W. "Student Evaluations of University Teaching: Research Findings, Methodological Issues, and Directions for Future Research." *International Journal of Educational Research,* 1987, 11, 253–388.

Murray, H. G. "Low-Inference Classroom Teaching Behaviors in Relation to Six Measures of College Teaching Effectiveness." Paper presented at the Conference on the Evaluation and Improvement of University Teaching, Montebello, Quebec, Canada, November 1983.

Ory, J. C., and Wieties, R. "A Longitudinal Study of Faculty Selection of ICES Student Evaluation Items." Paper presented at the 75th annual meetings of the American Educational Research Association, Chicago, April 1991.

Theall, M., and Franklin, J. "Student Ratings in the Context of Complex Evaluation Systems." In M. Theall and J. Franklin (eds.), *Student Ratings of Instruction: Issues for Improving Practice.* New Directions for Teaching and Learning, no. 43. San Francisco: Jossey-Bass, 1990.

Theall, M., and Franklin, J. "A Low-Threat, High-Impact Method of Developing a Student Ratings Questionnaire in a Department or College." Workshop presented at the 12th annual sharing conference of the Southern Regional Faculty and Instructional Development Consortium, Atlanta, Georgia, February 1991.

Michael Theall is associate professor and director of the Teaching and Learning Center at the School of Education, University of Alabama, Birmingham.

Jennifer Franklin is associate director for evaluation and senior research associate in the Office of Instructional Research and Evaluation of the Center for Applied Social Research at Northeastern University, Boston, Massachusetts.

Part Three

The Human Resources of Teaching

Studies of teaching effectiveness have concentrated on the measurable direct outcomes of instruction: students' satisfaction (as measured by ratings) and learning (as measured by tests and grades). These studies have omitted an important part of the teaching effectiveness picture: the relationship between teaching and job satisfaction of the instructor.

Incorporating Job Satisfaction into a Model of Instructional Effectiveness

Patricia Cranton, Robert Knoop

In this chapter we describe a model of instructional effectiveness that incorporates the instructor's job satisfaction, we integrate and summarize the literature supporting the model, and we discuss the model's implications for making decisions about instructional effectiveness and improvement as well as for conducting research on instructional effectiveness. Research on the effectiveness of instruction in higher education has been conducted for over thirty years, largely through empirical studies using student ratings forms. Educators have attempted to define the dimensions or factors of teaching, and comprehensive and critical reviews of this research have been provided by Feldman (1977), Marsh (1987), and Abrami (1985), among others. But many studies on instructional effectiveness have been limited. For example, results have been dependent on specific evaluation instruments that were not based on a theory or model of teaching, early research used an inappropriate unit of analysis (individual students within classes or pooled across classes), the outcomes of teaching effectiveness (cognitive and affective student learning) have been largely ignored, and the context in which instruction takes place (course and learner characteristics) has only rarely been related to the dimensions of teaching, even though the effect of course characteristics on student ratings has been studied extensively.

As Abrami (1985, p. 224) states, "The question should not be 'What is the ideal college teacher?' but rather 'What is the ideal college teacher for different contexts (i.e., courses, students, and settings) and different goals, objectives or desired outcomes of instruction?' " Progress toward a fuller understanding of the nature of instructional effectiveness will not be made until a comprehensive model of instruction can provide a basis for developing instruments, guiding practitioners, and generating research hypotheses. But even Abrami's question does not include the issue of faculty satisfaction with teaching, with career, and with working environment, although these issues have been addressed in discussions of faculty stress, burnout, and careers (see, for example, Chapter Eight of this volume; Machell, 1988-1989; Seldin, 1987; Sorcinelli, 1989).

Machell (1989) lists three stages of "professorial melancholia." In the early stage, symptoms include resentment of students, frustration, discouragement, and withdrawal. In the middle stage, these symptoms increase in intensity and frequency and are joined by decreases in self-esteem, diminished scholarly interest, and criticalness and an increase in feelings that work has become hurtful and repetitious drudgery. In the late stage (in which manifestations such as alcohol and drug abuse, interrelationship problems, verbal and grade abuse of students often arise), the list of symptoms includes deep alienation, arrogance, intense cynicism, and the feeling that students are enemies. How can such feelings not affect teaching effectiveness? And, equally important, is it reasonable to assume that relief of these problems will have a direct and positive effect on teaching? There is not much research that provides empirical evidence of this intuitively compelling proposition, although Boice's success (see Chapter Eight) with early intervention and Doyle's suggestions (see Chapter Nine) for treatment of faculty provide some promising approaches.

A Model of Instructional Effectiveness

This chapter proposes a model of teaching effectiveness that includes both job satisfaction and personal characteristics of the instructor. Our intent is to provide a framework for decisions, actions, and research on teaching effectiveness and improvement. The model of instructional effectiveness depicted in Figure 7.1 is based on an analysis and integration of the literature. The model contains three general components: personal characteristics (of instructor and learner), contextual variables (course characteristics, working conditions, and instructional strategies), and outcomes (teaching effectiveness, instructor job satisfaction, and student learning).

Instructor and learner characteristics, separately and in concert, influence choices of instructional strategies. The personal characteristics of the instructor may include psychological type, teaching style, experience, subject knowledge, job motivation, and job involvement. Similarly, the characteristics of the learner may include psychological type, learning style and earlier learning experiences, previous knowledge, perceived difficulty of the subject, motivation, and effort expended on learning.

Instructional strategies are perceived to influence teaching effectiveness, and two sets of variables are expected to affect or moderate these

Figure 7.1. A Model of Instructional Effectiveness

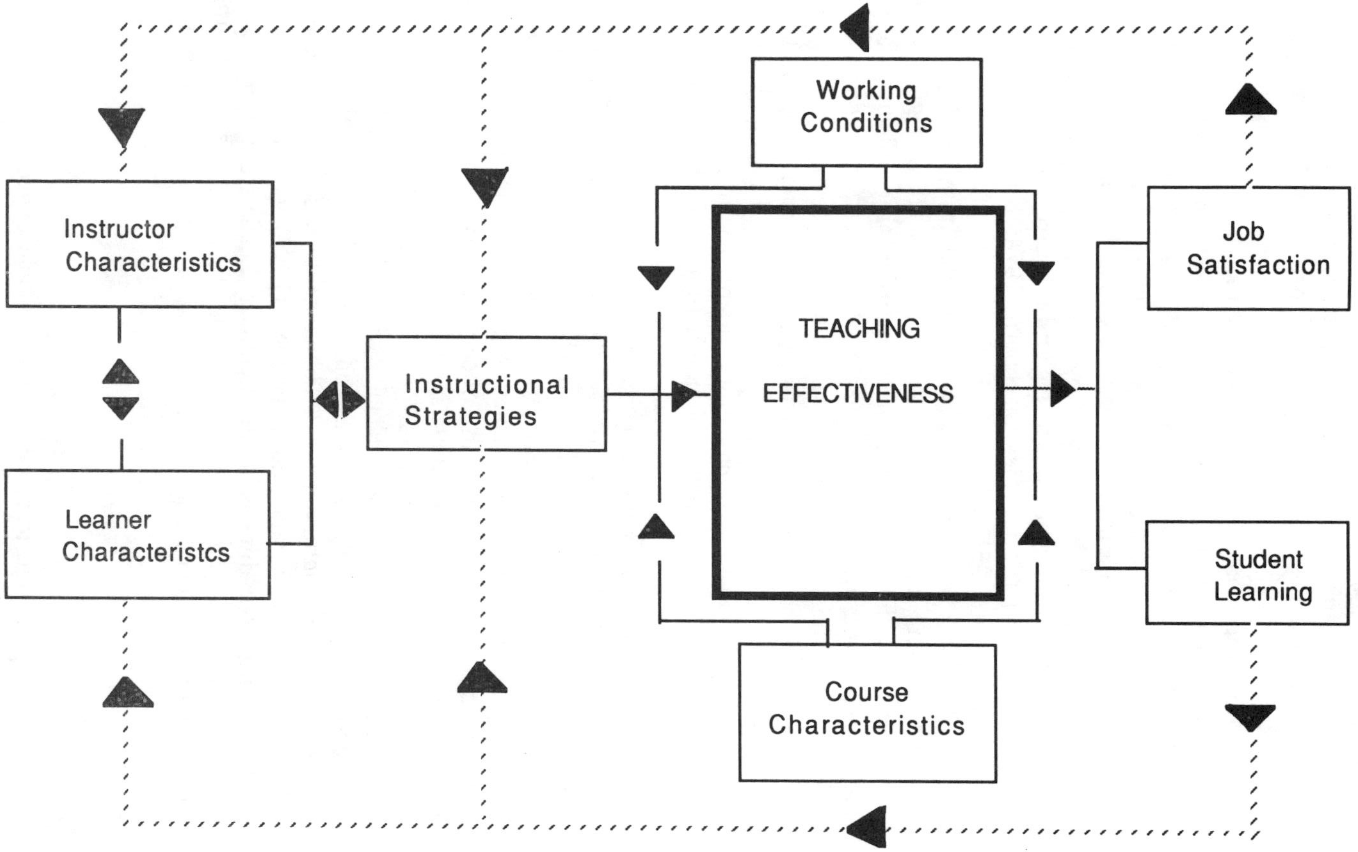

relationships: working conditions (such as time of day, physical facilities, availability of resources, and the reward system for teaching) and course characteristics (such as size of class, level of instruction, and discipline of subject taught).

Teaching effectiveness, then, is conceived as the product of instructor and learner characteristics, working conditions, course characteristics, and instructional strategies employed in a specific setting. However, effectiveness cannot be validated without the second-level outcomes (students' cognitive and affective learning and instructor satisfaction with the process of teaching) for these are influenced by teaching effectiveness. Successful teaching should lead to student learning and to instructor satisfaction with the work and with the job (see Blackburn, 1974; Blackburn, Horowitz, Edington, and Klos, 1986).

The feedback loops included in the model indicate that effective instruction is not a unidirectional process. As depicted in Figure 7.1, the lower portion of the loop shows that student learning influences learner characteristics and instructional strategies: As the student gains in knowledge and skills, different strategies and methods can be employed in teaching. Instructional strategies also affect learner characteristics; the learner who is required to be self-directed, for example, will change from being instructor-dependent to instructor-independent. The upper portion of the feedback loop shows that instructor satisfaction with job and work influences instructor characteristics, such as increased self-esteem and improved mental and physical health.

The model illustrates the complexity of the teaching and learning process and explains, in part, the difficulties that have been encountered in conducting research on the evaluation of instruction. The model is based largely on research into evaluation of instruction that has used student rating data. The three main concerns of evaluation literature have been reliability, validity, and dimensionality, and findings in these areas have been consistent. Feldman (1977), Marsh (1987), and many others have reported that ratings are reliable, while Cohen's (1981) work with multisection validity studies has established the positive relationship of ratings and student achievement. Dimensionality has been addressed by Feldman (1976) and Abrami and d'Apollonia (1990), who reported twenty-one and twenty-four dimensions, respectively. Readers are encouraged to consult comprehensive reviews (for example, Abrami, 1985; Marsh, 1987) for details of this literature and their implications for practice (Theall and Franklin, 1990).

Job Satisfaction

If teaching is perceived to be effective, one would expect favorable faculty attitudes toward the job of teaching (that is, job satisfaction). Two aspects of job satisfaction are generally differentiated: an overall attitude toward the job and specific feelings about various facets of job satisfaction (for example, the tendency to be more or less satisfied with teaching itself, with students and co-workers, with opportunities for advancement, and with pay). Since attitudes are derived from the product of associated beliefs and values, they are related to differences in perceptions of job satisfaction (even when two jobs are identical) and to what individuals want from their jobs. These correlates of job satisfaction can be related to discrepancy theory (Locke, 1976), where satisfaction is a function of the discrepancy between desired and perceived job outcomes. For example, an instructor who likes interaction with students, but who, due to large class sizes, is required to lecture, would be dissatisfied with that aspect of the job.

If teaching effectiveness is marginal, job satisfaction can also be expected to be the same. With improved teaching, satisfaction with the work and with the job overall should increase. This satisfaction, in turn, should have a positive effect on absenteeism, turnover, tardiness, and several general factors such as life satisfaction, self-confidence, and general mental health. Similarly, effective teaching facilitates student learning and various positive, internal responses such as higher self-esteem and a more internal locus of control, as well as increased chances of success in employment or future academic situations.

Second-level outcomes, such as instructor job satisfaction, have rarely been included in the research on instructional effectiveness. The literature specifically related to instructor job satisfaction in higher education contains a limited number of investigations (Stevens, 1988; Knoop, 1986; Levanoni and Knoop, 1985; Pearson and Seiler, 1983). Unfortunately, none of these studies has linked this variable to instructional effectiveness.

Likewise, programs in faculty/instructional development and teaching improvement rarely consider job satisfaction. In this volume, George Geis's, Robert Menges's, and Kathleen Brinko's comments about faculty perspective illuminate the point that it is unwarranted to expect improvement from programs that focus on teaching skills if the problems at hand are not pedagogical. Faculty who are dissatisfied with their jobs will not be receptive to suggestions that, in effect, ask them to spend more time on their teaching.

Implications for Improving Teaching

The starting point for improvement is most often an evaluation of teaching effectiveness, but any single, standard rating form is unlikely to be appropriate for every individual. Instructors should have the opportunity to select items that are relevant to their own settings, strategies, and learners. To ensure that evaluation is comprehensive, consultation or even written guidelines may be needed. In practice, unfortunately, individual faculty most often borrow rating forms from colleagues and administer them to students; but when they find the responses difficult to interpret, they file the results. At best, departments or faculties often have only one general form available for evaluation. It is rare for instructors to go through the systematic planning of an evaluation procedure appropriate to their own instructional setting, even though this procedure is clearly the most useful for teaching improvement.

Different teaching skills are likely to have varying "value" or importance in different contexts in terms of teaching effectiveness. The literature indicates that organizational skills are the best predictors of teaching effectiveness in some settings, whereas in other settings discussion-leading skills are the best predictors of overall effectiveness (Cranton and Smith, 1986). What the instructor most often does with the results of student ratings is select the items with the lowest ratings as areas in need of improvement. This, in fact, is also often the approach taken by instructional developers. However, it may well be that those items are not related to effectiveness in a particular setting and that the improvement efforts are, therefore, not meaningful. As clarified in our model, the entire instructional setting needs to be considered in the development of improvement strategies. Although this strategy sounds exceedingly complex, it can be quite a simple procedure for an individual or a department to implement. All rating forms can include a number of "overall effectiveness" items (for example, overall teaching quality, course quality, and amount learned). A basic computer program can provide correlations of specific skill items with the overall ratings. Those skills that have the highest correlations are most likely to be the important or valued skills in that particular setting. The instructor can then use both importance and student responses in selecting the teaching areas that need improvement. The advantage of this process is that it relates more closely to faculty needs and interests and is thus more congruent with faculty perceptions and values. As Geis, Menges, and Brinko point out in their respective chapters of this volume, the individual must value both the process and its emphases in order for change to take place.

Finally, the use of different sources of information is as important for decisions about teaching improvement as it is for promotion and tenure decisions. Student ratings may provide reasonable assessments of most classroom behaviors, but they are not necessarily useful in describing components of instruction (for example, instructor expertise and preparation, currency of materials, and match between instructor characteristics and context). Peer reviews of material, anecdotal comments, reviews of student products, and interviews or discussions with graduates or dropouts can all provide valuable perspectives on teaching and yield a comprehensive picture of an individual's strengths and weaknesses. The counterargument here is usually that these techniques are too time-consuming. Yet, when one considers the faculty time spent in preparing for class and working with learners, the time spent in evaluating the quality of teaching is surely not out of place.

Implications for Other Decisions About Teaching

The most common evaluation-based, administrative decisions made about teaching in higher education relate to promotion and tenure and to program evaluation. The assignment of instructors to courses could also be based on evaluative information, but usually it is not. The following sections of this chapter consider the implications of job satisfaction with respect to administrative decisions, program evaluation, course assignments, and research on teaching effectiveness.

Promotion and Tenure Decisions. Student ratings are generally the primary source of information for promotion and tenure decisions. In the model presented here, these ratings reflect only one part of one component of second-level outcomes and do not reveal anything about several other contributing components. It has been argued (Centra, 1979; Cranton, 1982) that evaluation of instructional effectiveness must include more than one source of information, but this standard is rarely observed in practice. In fact, nearly all of the research on instructional effectiveness is based on student rating data. Other indicators of teaching quality must be included to yield a more comprehensive picture. These include instructor satisfaction, student learning, independent observations of instructional strategies, and peer review of teaching strategies. In addition, the course characteristics and the conditions under which the instructor works have to be considered in any description of teaching. Further, peers and supervisors could be asked to observe and rate instructional effectiveness to supplement student ratings and self-ratings.

Program Evaluation. Evaluations of instructional programs are more likely to include information other than student ratings. Several good comprehensive models of program evaluation exist (see Scriven, 1967) and are utilized by administrators. However, some of the same pitfalls experienced in teaching evaluation still exist here. Comparisons are often made between programs in an attempt to decide which format is "more beneficial" and therefore which format should be kept and which should be discarded. A college, for example, may have to decide whether a modularized program or a classroom program should be used in academic upgrading. This kind of decision is often based on comparisons of student learning or on student and instructor perceptions of quality. Once again, comparisons made of one or two variables cannot be valid. Even the inevitable variation in one component of the model, learner characteristics, yields a meaningless "difference" between formats. Criteria that are independent of other programs must be developed in order to make a choice; such criteria could be based, for example, on institutional goals or cost-effectiveness. A parallel can be found here in the last eighty years of methods-comparison research (discussion versus lecture, computerized versus traditional, and so on), where consistent differences have not been found because individual differences among learners and instructors have only rarely been considered.

While promotion and tenure decisions tend to rely heavily on student ratings, program evaluations tend to overemphasize student learning as a basis for decision making. Quite often, a variable such as student grades is used to make program decisions. And yet it is clear that student learning is but one component of instructional effectiveness and that it is influenced by a host of other variables. Once again, more than one source of information must be utilized in describing the quality of any instruction.

Course Assignments. Assignment of courses is typically done by a chairperson or program director and is based on the instructor's academic expertise as well as on practical constraints such as the timetable. However, if we consider that instructor, learner, and course characteristics and working conditions interact with each other to influence teaching effectiveness, these variables should be considered in course assignment decisions. For example, an instructor whose personality and background is most effective in small graduate seminars should be assigned to this setting rather than "rotated through" a variety of undergraduate courses, as is often done. Other faculty are likely to be more suited to the "authority" role or the "entertainer" role and are therefore more effective in large, lecture-style settings. Such strategies offset the tendency to seek "fairness" in rotations of course assignments. A more appropriate approach is to base course assignments on careful evaluation of teaching effectiveness in different contexts and to consider as many variables as possible in matching instructor to course.

Research on Teaching Effectiveness. Previous research on instructional effectiveness has not been either theory or model based but rather has been derived from analyses of student ratings. Recently, researchers have indicated the need for a theoretical framework in which to pursue further study (Abrami, 1985). The model presented in this chapter can be used to generate a variety of hypotheses.

Learner and instructor characteristics, individually and jointly, are hypothesized to predict type and frequency of use of instructional strategies. The use of instructor-centered methods (for example, lecture or demonstration) or interactive methods (discussion groups or group activities) is related to instructor characteristics such as personality type, internal motivation, values, and knowledge of and familiarity with various teaching styles. The choice of strategies is also related to learner characteristics such as degree of self-directedness, previous experience, and locus of control. Instructor-centered strategies are likely to be preferred by those instructors who know only this one method and who are not motivated enough to explore other methods, and by those students who lack self-initiative, have had no experience with interactive methods, or hold an external locus of control. If both instructors and students value discussion, debate, and dialectical inquiry, the preferred instructional strategy is likely to be interactive.

Instructional strategies (as influenced by learner and instructor characteristics) in turn predict the dimensions of teaching effectiveness; that is, depending on the individuals involved in the teaching and learning process, different instructional strategies are more or less effective. A thinking-type instructor who uses logical argument to lecture a group of feeling-type learners is not likely to be perceived as effective. By definition, feeling types do not prefer didactic methods or logical argumentation as a way of learning (Jung, 1971). However, such predictions are moderated by both working conditions and course characteristics. Variables such as time of day, physical facilities, size of class, discipline, and level of instruction influence the relationship between instructional methods and teaching effectiveness. Interaction strategies are not perceived as effective when the class size is large and the classroom is small, even if both instructors and learners prefer this strategy.

In our model, teaching effectiveness predicts two second-level outcomes: student learning and instructor job satisfaction. Instructors who receive positive feedback on their teaching are likely to be more satisfied with their jobs and with the work that they are performing. High job satisfaction, "a pleasurable or positive emotional state resulting from the appraisal of one's job or job experiences" (Locke, 1976, p. 300), occurs when work is congruent with the instructor's needs and values. Similarly, students who perceive teaching as effective are likely to have learned more than students who perceive teaching as ineffective.

The relationship between teaching effectiveness and the two second-level outcomes is likely to be moderated by working conditions and course characteristics. Even teaching that is perceived as effective does not lead to high instructor satisfaction if the room is too hot or overcrowded. Students who have to sit on the floor and cannot take adequate notes may give the instructor high ratings but may well feel that part of the material has eluded them.

The feedback loops in Figure 7.1 indicate that second-level outcomes influence antecedent variables. Student learning influences learner characteristics and instructional strategies. If students receive high grades that they feel are deserved, their self-esteem and confidence are likely to increase, and they may seek out instructors who employ strategies that have led to such success. Instructors' feelings of efficacy and expectancy for successful outcomes also increase when they consider their work satisfying, and they will likely seek out similar teaching situations.

We should point out that while Figure 7.1 depicts an apparently closed system, the model presented here is not truly closed. In fact, instructional effectiveness is deeply embedded in the overall college environment and is both responsive to and affected by it. A significant rise or decline in teaching effectiveness affects the institution just as support from the institution affects the impact and success of teaching improvement efforts.

Clearly, there is no straightforward or linear relationship among the many variables that are the antecedents or the outcomes of teaching effectiveness. Researchers must work with this complexity and yet try to validate a model of instructional effectiveness that is of use to instructors, administrators, and instructional developers alike.

References

Abrami, P. C. "Dimensions of Effective College Instruction." *Review of Higher Education,* 1985, *8,* 211–228.

Abrami, P. C., and d'Apollonia, S. "The Dimensionality of Ratings and Their Use in Personnel Decisions." In M. Theall and J. Franklin (eds.), *Student Ratings of Instruction: Issues for Improving Practice.* New Directions for Teaching and Learning, no. 43. San Francisco: Jossey-Bass, 1990.

Blackburn, R. T. "The Meaning of Work in Academia." In J. I. Doi (ed.), *Assessing Faculty Effort.* San Francisco: Jossey-Bass, 1974.

Blackburn, R. T., Horowitz, S. M., Edington, D. W., and Klos, D. M. "University Faculty and Administrator Response to Stresses: Correlations with Health and Job/Life Satisfaction." *Research in Higher Education,* 1986, *25* (1), 31–41.

Centra, J. A. *Determining Faculty Effectiveness: Assessing Teaching, Research, and Service for Personnel Decisions and Improvement.* San Francisco: Jossey-Bass, 1979.

Cohen, P. A. "Student Ratings of Instruction and Student Achievement: A Meta-Analysis of Multisection Validity Studies." *Review of Educational Research,* 1981, *51,* 281–309.

Cranton, P. A. *McGill Evaluation System: User Guide.* Montréal, Québec, Canada: Center for Teaching and Learning Services, 1982.

Cranton, P. A., and Smith, R. "A New Look at the Effect of Course Characteristics on Student Ratings of Instruction." *American Educational Research Journal,* 1986, *23,* 117–128.

Feldman, K. "The Superior College Teacher from the Students' View." *Research in Higher Education,* 1976, *5,* 243–288.

Feldman, K. "Consistency and Variability Among College Students in Rating Their Teachers and Courses." *Research in Higher Education,* 1977, *6,* 223–274.

Jung, C. *Psychological Types.* Princeton, N.J.: Princeton University Press, 1971.

Knoop, R. "Causes of Alienation Among University Professors." *Perceptual and Motor Skills,* 1986, *63,* 677–678.

Levanoni, E., and Knoop, R. "Does Task Structure Moderate the Relationship of Leaders' Behavior and Employees' Satisfaction?" *Psychological Reports,* 1985, *57,* 611–623.

Locke, E. A. "Nature and Causes of Job Satisfaction." In M. D. Dunnette (ed.), *Handbook of Industrial and Organizational Psychology.* Skokie, Ill.: Rand McNally, 1976.

Machell, D. F. "A Discourse on Professorial Melancholia." *Community Review,* 1988–1989, *9* (1–2), 41–50.

Marsh, H. "Students' Evaluations of University Teaching: Research Findings, Methodological Issues, and Directions for Future Research." *International Journal of Educational Research,* 1987, *11,* 253–388.

Pearson, D., and Seiler, R. "Environmental Satisfiers in Academe." *Higher Education,* 1983, *12,* 35–47.

Scriven, M. "The Methodology of Evaluation." In R. W. Tyler, R. M. Gagne, and M. Scriven (eds.), *Perspectives of Curriculum Evaluation*. Skokie, Ill.: Rand McNally, 1967.

Seldin, P. (ed.). *Coping with Faculty Stress*. New Directions for Teaching and Learning, no. 29. San Francisco: Jossey-Bass, 1987.

Sorcinelli, M. D. "Relations Between Work and Life Away from Work Among University Faculty." *Journal of Higher Education*, 1989, 60 (1), 59–81.

Stevens, E. "Tinkering with Teaching." *Review of Higher Education*, 1988, 12, 63–78.

Theall, M., and Franklin, J. (eds.). *Student Ratings of Instruction: Issues for Improving Practice*. New Directions for Teaching and Learning, no. 43. San Francisco: Jossey-Bass, 1990.

Patricia Cranton is professor in the Faculty of Education at Brock University, St. Catharines, Ontario, Canada.

Robert Knoop is professor in the Faculty of Education at Brock University, St. Catharines, Ontario, Canada.

Some faculty find their working situations and their careers to be energizing and productive. Others are frustrated, unproductive, and will "burn out" quickly, leaving behind a trail of effort without success and ill feelings toward their institutions and the professoriate. What are the differences between these two types and can we capitalize on the skills and working styles of the "quick starters" to help those less fortunate?

Quick Starters: New Faculty Who Succeed

Robert Boice

Most of what we know about how professors teach comes from studies of already experienced teachers. As a result, we understand little about how teaching is learned or about why some of us master it more readily than do others.

This chapter demonstrates a simple strategy for identifying new faculty who make quick starts and it suggests that we can profit in comparing them to other new hires. The result is a new way of looking at instructional improvement, based on communication of the basics of teaching that work so impressively for "quick starters."

Normative Behaviors of New Faculty as Teachers

In a decade of studying new faculty as teachers, I have made a point of interviewing a whole range of colleagues, even those who would ordinarily avoid faculty development programs. The advantage in this patient style, beyond the eventual rapport it builds, is its potential for uncovering aspects of teaching that faculty ordinarily do not verbalize. For example, when new faculty were interviewed and observed over several successive semesters (see Boice, 1991, for details), they revealed some striking commonalities about how most professors start as teachers. As the following list shows, many of the initial habits of new faculty seem less than ideal:

1. Most new faculty, even those who had taught at other campuses, tended to teach in a facts-and-principles style of lecturing (Fink, 1984). As a rule, new faculty equated good teaching with good content. Almost without exception in my sample, new faculty volunteered plans to teach in

more interactive styles, but not until they felt comfortable as teachers. Curiously, new faculty with considerable prior teaching experience admitted that they had rarely strayed from familiar patterns of lecturing.

2. Most new faculty taught defensively, with the specific aim of avoiding complaints made by students to senior colleagues, especially chairpeople. New faculty at all three study campuses showed an awareness that such complaints, once registered in retention/tenure/promotion reports, could persist and become reasons for termination. Almost invariably, new faculty tried to defend themselves against this potential danger by focusing on content (what they called "getting their facts straight"); the most indefensible criticism imaginable to them was not knowing their lecture material. Incidentally, new faculty almost never worried about the kinds of factors that faculty developers typically assume are critical to excellence in teaching, such as displaying enthusiasm for teaching and assessing student learning.

3. The majority of these few hundred new faculty under study received student evaluations that fell well below their expectations,. As a rule, they blamed these mediocre-to-poor ratings on external factors such as the quality of students, teaching loads, invalid rating systems, and class times and sizes.

4. Few new faculty planned improvements as teachers beyond making their lecture notes better organized and error-free.

5. New faculty's most important goal as teachers, a priority revealed only after several semesters of contacts, was to get to the point where teaching no longer took as much time to prepare or as much emotion to conduct. That is, they looked forward to lecture preparation that would not dominate work weeks and to classes where they would feel comfortable. New faculty in their first three years at large campuses expended surprising amounts of time in lecture preparation: Norms for new faculty with two-course-per-semester assignments were thirteen to twenty-two hours per week; with three-course loads, eighteen to twenty-seven hours. One result of this pattern was busyness and stressfulness (Boice, 1989). Another result was a growing aversion to teaching as an activity that took too much time and paid too few rewards.

6. By their own admission, new faculty typically went to class overprepared; that is, they prepared so much to say that they had to rush to say it all. In so doing, they inadvertently discouraged students from active participation in classes.

7. Most new faculty established comfort, efficiency, and student acceptance slowly, if at all, during my two to four years of regular contact with them. Even by the fourth year the majority of inexperienced new faculty reported feeling tense, worrying about not being in control of classes and doubting that students liked them.

Overall, this is a disheartening pattern, one that probably holds true on a variety of campuses. Its generality is easily enough tested. But even where practitioners are not inclined to carry out systematic research, they can profit in interviewing enough new faculty to identify some of the quick starters on campus. These exemplary newcomers provide important relief from the discouraging beginnings of most professors. Moreover, quick starters may suggest simple strategies for enhancing the performance of other teachers.

Characteristics of Quick Starters

So far, my colleagues and I have identified inexperienced new faculty as quick starters, usually during their second and third semesters on campus, when they scored in the top quartile on these dimensions: (1) classroom observers' ratings of new faculty's teaching in terms of classroom comfort, rapport with students, and student involvement, (2) students' ratings of teaching in formal, end-of-semester evaluations and in early, informal evaluations (Boice, 1990a), and (3) new faculty's self-ratings of their enjoyment and comfort as teachers. At the three campuses where quick starters are under study, the incidence of new faculty who meet these criteria is 5 to 9 percent. Incidentally, the rate at which experienced new hires (that is, those with considerable prior teaching) meet these criteria is somewhat lower.

Thus far, eight concomitants of quick starts have proven reliable. Overall, the twenty-two quick starters observed for at least a year (usually during their second and third semesters on campus) showed the following, relatively unique tendencies:

1. They lectured in a facts-and-principles style but in a comfortable fashion that allowed time for student involvement. This more relaxed pacing included verbal and nonverbal cues that encouraged students to participate.
2. They verbalized (to me) uncritical, accepting, and optimistic attitudes about the undergraduate students on their campuses.
3. They displayed low levels of complaining and cynicism about their campuses and their colleagues in terms of supportiveness and competence.
4. They showed a marked disposition to seek advice about teaching, from colleagues, via reading and observing, and from faculty development programs. Specifically, they spent an average of four hours per week in social contacts with colleagues that included discussions about teaching.
5. They evidenced quick transitions away from spending the bulk of work weeks on teaching preparation, usually by the end of the first semester on campus. Specifically, they settled into patterns of work allocation that typically included no more than one and one-half hours of preparation per classroom hour by the third semester.
6. They produced a documented balance of time expenditures among aca-

demic activities so that at least three hours per week (of at least half the weeks during semesters) were spent on scholarly writing by the second semester. Accordingly, quick starters were nearly unique in producing scholarly outputs at levels consistent with tenure standards on their campuses (mean = 1.5 published manuscripts per year). (Recall that, by definition, quick starters also excel as teachers during their first year on campus.)

7. They integrated their research and scholarly interests into undergraduate classes, resulting in enthusiasm for teaching and recruitment of students as research assistants.
8. They displayed high energy, broad interests (for example, singing in choirs), concern with self-presentation, and a sense of humor (see Cole, 1986, for a similar finding).

What can we learn from the pattern just outlined? The obvious answers relate to the greater skill of quick starters in establishing moderation in lecture preparation, in meeting other academic needs including collegiality and scholarly productivity, and in finding comfort with their classes, their students, their colleagues, and their campuses. All in all, quick starters seemed to be more positive, more sociable, and more efficient individuals. A problem in stating the differences from other new faculty in this way is that it can discourage emulation; quick starters may seem like gifted people who are necessarily exceptions.

My own thinking about what makes quick starters different keeps drifting back to my interests in understanding success at writing. There are also quick starters among professorial writers and they display illuminating similarities to quick starters as teachers. Briefly, quick starters as writers, unlike their relatively silent colleagues, postpone attention to the *process* and *product* of writing, concentrating first on regular *practice* and *comfort* as writers.

This postponement of addressing product (final outcomes in terms of writing quality) and process (finding ways to write for an audience, with flow and voice) actually increases the likelihood that writers will eventually deal with process and product (Tremmel, 1989). That is, quick starters begin by establishing the mind set and habits of already productive writers, by working at writing regularly, regardless of readiness (Boice, 1990b). Then, once underway, they seek out related solutions to process and product in a timely and enthusiastic fashion.

Quick starters as teachers, similarly, put off the usual concerns of new faculty about product (for example, the completeness of their lecture notes) and process (for example, attempts to abandon lecturing for discussion-based classes). Instead, they begin by attending to issues of practice in comfortable and efficient fashion. Specifically, they talk about wanting to begin with comfort in the classroom, with acceptance and feedback from students, and with enough time left over to take care of other essential needs such as establishing collegial networks and scholarly productivity. Then, much like quick starters as writers, they build a practical and timely interest in the process and product of teaching once productive practice is underway.

The point in drawing this parallel between quick starters as writers and quick starters as teachers is that, in both cases, the habits, intellectual skills, and attitudes that distinguish these exemplary new hires are basic and teachable. Sternberg and his colleagues call this sort of practical intelligence *tacit knowledge* and conclude that it is rarely taught but nonetheless very teachable (Sternberg, Okagaki, and Jackson, 1990). In fact, much evidence already exists to show that academic writers can profit from emulating the simple basics of quick starters (see, for example, Boice, 1989). In this chapter, the emphasis is on emulating the practices of quick starters as teachers.

Testing the First-Factor Rule with Slower Starters

There is, of course, nothing new about suggesting that new faculty should include the most basic skills in their initial efforts at mastering teaching; the most successful guide for teachers emphasizes basics such as monitoring student note taking as an index of their comprehension (McKeachie, 1986). What may be novel, however, is the notion that new teachers fare best when they address certain basics first.

As a preliminary test of this idea, I have begun studies where slower starters are coached to imitate quick starters. Results of ongoing studies with fifteen new faculty at two campuses indicate that at least some of the practices of quick starters are promising as interventions for other new faculty. In fact, we opted to initiate our program with what quick starters themselves suggested would assist most: helping colleagues find balance in time expenditures. (This is not, I suspect, where I would have embarked on my own, at least in regard to facilitation of teaching.)

Thus, we recruited new faculty who had established clearly distressing beginnings as teachers to participate in a "balance program." These participants represented a wide cross section of faculty who agreed to remain involved for at least an academic year and to (1) keep daily, verifiable records of how they spent their work time (Boice, 1987), (2) decrease classroom preparation to a maximum of two hours per classroom hour, (3) increase social networking aimed at supporting teaching and scholarship, (4) increase time spent on scholarly writing to thirty to sixty minutes per workday, regardless of readiness to write, and (5) integrate their own research and scholarly interests into lectures.

While participants invariably expected these assignments to be difficult and time-consuming, the eventual result was quite different. This uncomplicated paradigm of helping new hires with the "first factor" in teaching—starting with the basics of comfortable and efficient practice before moving to process and product—brought uniform comments about increases in the ease of working and in free time for nonwork.

Tentative Results

The key ingredient in the quick starters program is time, or, more specifically, management of one's time to provide balance among three major areas: preparation for teaching, collegial interactions, and writing. For new faculty, this time management means avoiding overpreparation, seeking dialogue about teaching and scholarship, and committing time to writing.

Preparation Time. The task of cutting back on preparation time was evidently the most difficult of all the changes requested from participants. As a rule, it elicited anxiety about going to class and feeling out of control. The following comment typifies those made by new faculty whom I accompanied to their classroom doors: "This feels risky. What if I draw a blank or what if I can't think of exactly what to say? I felt a whole lot better when I took the time to write out *everything* in advance. Now I'm not sure exactly how I'll say everything. I don't want to look foolish."

Eight participants mastered this step on the basis of what they termed a "leap of faith." They simply went in without having points completely written out in advance; their main goal was to be spontaneous but careful in presenting materials clearly. Five others did not make the transition until they observed one or two quick starters who demonstrated the technique of improvising around a clear structure (for example, an outline on the board or a handout) and of relying on students for some of the explanations and solutions in their own classes. The other two participants proved especially resistant to the change but took the risk of going to class "imperfectly prepared" after I coached them through role plays with small groups of supportive colleagues acting as students.

Two more components complete this tentative picture. First, once in the mode of going to class with moderate preparation, the new faculty invariably reported feeling more at ease. Their students enjoyed the greater spontaneity of presentation and of participation. And the new faculty noted that they left class less exhausted and more satisfied than before. Second, the new faculty's concerns about becoming "lazy preparers" once they learned to teach more spontaneously proved unfounded. Instead, they continued to prepare enough to bring clear structure, definite learning goals (something new for them), and plans for flexibility to class.

So far, proof of the effectiveness of this intervention has been essentially limited to improvements in the early, informal student evaluations of participants (Boice, 1990a), in end-of-semester student ratings, and in the new faculty's self-ratings. In terms of these indices, at least, students and faculty see their classes as more comfortable, interactive, and instructive.

Socialization Time. The requested increase in time allotted for the establishment of support networks was initially resisted, usually for reasons of busyness. Socialization seemed to be an activity that could wait until the new faculty had more time. Resistance also came in the form of concerns about sources of contacts; the participants were ready to suppose that they knew too few potential contacts and that colleagues worth soliciting would feel imposed upon. Practice proved otherwise.

Here again, the strategies of inducing leaps of faith, of modeling, and of role playing successfully induced involvement. Once involved, participants reported that this socialization time was the most enjoyable aspect of their work weeks; documented benefits included advice about practice and opportunities for collaboration in writing and in teaching.

Writing Time. Here too, the new faculty reported feeling unprepared to begin, despite agreeing that writing was critical to their survival and development. The essential problem was to move them past preconceptions about the need to find large blocks of undisrupted time for writing. But once they agreed to try approximations to manuscript writing in brief daily sessions (Boice, 1990b), the value of beginning before feeling ready and of getting something done amidst busy workdays was apparent.

Much like their colleagues designated as quick starters, these new faculty evidenced an average of about three hours of writing per week (compared to an average of twenty-four minutes per week for other new faculty). Equally important, in the view of participants, the increase in the amount of writing done was a boon to their general sense of well-being and coincided with an end to resentment of teaching as an interfering activity.

Implications and Applications

At first glance, the first-factor rule has promise for facilitating teaching. The first factor appears to be an important component in the success of quick starters, and it evidently works when transferred to the habit patterns of slower starters. We may find it easier to consider adoption of this seemingly unusual idea upon seeing its roots in already familiar notions of instructional development.

Kinship Patterns. A striking quality of quick starters and of compensated slow starters is the interest they show in learning more about teaching (Cole, 1986). In many ways, they reflect what Cross and Angelo (1988) call *classroom research*. That is, quick starters, whether spontaneous or converted, actively collect data from their own and their students' experiences as part of making teaching easier. And then they take another step. Quick starters show a special interest in learning what their most successful colleagues do. This typical comment from a quick starter makes the point: "The more I get into this, the more I realize how much I have to learn. I'm fascinated to imagine all the clever ways that master teachers have devised to make teaching easier. They may not be used to verbalizing their savvy, but I'll bet that they can if stimulated by somebody who shares their fundamental excitement for teaching."

A second instance where first-factor thinking finds roots in common practice is in its emphasis on starting with the simplest, most basic elements of teaching. Quick starters make the explicit assumption that the most important keys to finding success as teachers are comfort and enjoyment. They even recognize that many of their colleagues, by virtue of their neglect of these basics, may be doomed to miserable beginnings and chronic disappointments with teaching. The pioneer in charting the experience of new faculty as teachers, Fink (in press, p. 7), observed a similarly unpromising start for those who "developed a teaching style in a time-shortened condition that had no time for creative reflection on how to teach effectively, no time to seek help in this regard, and no prospects for improvement of their time situation."

There is a literature on the importance of starting with basics. Appropriately, most of these beginnings occur within the boundaries of teaching assistant (TA) training. Consider this sampling: One correlate of improved student evaluations is an increase in the teacher's awareness of the affective components of classroom behavior (Abbott, Wulff, and Szego, 1989). Once TAs are comfortable enough to perceive and act on subtle student feedback, they fare better as teachers. Similarly, TAs, no matter what their styles as beginners, prefer personal guidance (mentoring) over instruction on the skills of teaching (Boehrer and Sarkisian, 1985). Stated another way, they want comfort before skills. The best TAs, in the view of their students, are those comfortable enough with students to avoid seeming too busy to help (Wulff, Nyquist, and Abbott, 1989). Finally, TAs who learn to interact in ready, friendly ways with students can overcome other obstacles to comfort and acceptance, including a lack of proficiency in speaking English (Bailey, 1983).

If, then, the first-factor rule generates a modicum of familiarity with the literature on instructional development and pedagogy, the next step is to outline its implications in more detail. A list of eight such implications is presented below.

1. Instructional development properly begins with concerns about comfortable and efficient practice, in contrast to traditional, premature emphases on process and product.
2. Most teachers, no matter how experienced, must resolve first-factor issues before they can make lasting progress in arenas of process (for example, supplanting lecturing with something else) or product (for example, student evaluations).

3. New faculty who begin amid their own and others' concerns for product (that is, avoidance of complaints and of bad ratings) may teach in a defensive, noninnovative fashion, perhaps permanently.
4. Effective, lasting instructional development cannot occur in isolation from collegial development and scholarly development.
5. As faculty confront issues of process and product, they will need to reestablish first-factor practices of comfortable and efficient practice. Without this link, process and product will have no basis for self-efficacious risk taking (Lucas, 1990) or for learning to get past disappointments with students (Tobias, 1990).
6. The first factor is rarely taught. Like many other kinds of practical intelligence, it is not explicitly tutored but is essential to success (Sternberg, Okagaki, and Jackson, 1990).
7. First-factor habits are apparently as amenable to learning as are the related factors tested by Sternberg, Okagaki, and Jackson (1990). In their view, the three essential components that teachers must master are self-management, task management (for example, balancing time), and social management.
8. Because first-factor practice encourages spontaneity, simultaneous activity in scholarly domains, and social inputs, one result should be more innovative and creative teaching.

Reflections About Application. In a way, the kind of information presented here can fall between the cracks in faculty development. This presentation of ideas about the first-factor rule may be too data-centered for practitioners who do not see themselves as prone to collect the repeated observations needed to draw the kinds of conclusions reached here.

But, like our new colleagues, we may fare better if we seek more balance among our activities and attitudes. Why can't we take time for some illuminating but imperfect data collection? Why shouldn't we assume that we have much to learn from the best teachers on campus, including those quick out of the gate? And, why must we exclude ourselves from the discovery process that goes into more formal research?

In conclusion, I suggest the following as starting points in the task of transporting ideas about the first-factor rule to other campuses: (1) Venture into the field and get to know a small sample of new faculty as they adapt to campus. New faculty welcome this attention during what is usually a lonely couple of years. (2) Solicit repeated and reflective observations (from new faculty and from one's own occasional and brief visits to their classrooms) about what distinguishes happy and successful teachers. (3) Compare other observations with mine. It may be that we can learn something about the effects of different campus cultures on what it takes to succeed at teaching. (4) Consider using information about quick starters in revising the instructional development programs at one's own campus (and recruiting quick starters as collaborators in coaching the basics of better teaching). (5) At the least, reconsider Lucas's (1990, p. 113) conclusion about what will most help faculty as teachers: Instead of worrying about *what* to say, they would do better to ask *how* they can present material in ways that create excitement about teaching.

References

Abbott, R. D., Wulff, D. H., and Szego, C. K. "Review of Research on TA Training." In J. D. Nyquist, R. D. Abbott, and D. H. Wulff (eds.), *Teaching Assistant Training in the 1990s.* New Directions for Teaching and Learning, no. 39. San Francisco: Jossey-Bass, 1989.

Boehrer, J., and Sarkisian, E. "The Teaching Assistant's Point of View." In J.D.W. Andrews (ed.), *Strengthening the Teaching Assistant Faculty.* New Directions for Teaching and Learning, no. 22. San Francisco: Jossey-Bass, 1985.

Boice, R. "Is Released Time an Effective Component of Faculty Development Programs?" *Research in Higher Education,* 1987, 26, 311–326.

Boice, R. "Procrastination, Busyness, and Bingeing." *Behaviour Research and Therapy,* 1989, 27, 605–611.

Boice, R. "Countering Common Misbeliefs About Student Evaluations of Teaching." *Teaching Excellence,* 1990a, 2 (2), 1–2.

Boice, R. *Professors as Writers.* Stillwater, Okla.: New Forums Press, 1990b.

Boice, R. "New Faculty as Teachers." *Journal of Higher Education,* 1991, 62 (2), 150–173.

Cole, D. L. "Attracting the Best and Brightest to Teach Psychology." *Teaching of Psychology,* 1986, 13 (3), 107–110.

Cross, K. P., and Angelo, T. A. *Classroom Assessment Techniques: A Handbook for Faculty.* Ann Arbor: National Center for Research to Improve Postsecondary Teaching and Learning, University of Michigan, 1988.

Fink, L. D. (ed.) *The First Year of College Teaching.* New Directions for Teaching and Learning, no. 17. San Francisco: Jossey-Bass, 1984.

Fink, L. D. "New Faculty Members: The Professoriate of Tomorrow." *Journal of Staff, Program, and Organization Development,* in press.

Lucas, A. F. "Using Psychological Models to Understand Student Motivation." In M. D. Svinicki (ed.), *The Changing Face of College Teaching.* New Directions for Teaching and Learning, no. 42. San Francisco: Jossey-Bass, 1990.

McKeachie, W. J. *Teaching Tips: A Guidebook for the Beginning College Teacher.* (8th ed.) Lexington, Mass.: Heath, 1986.

Sternberg, R. J., Okagaki, L., and Jackson, A. S. "Practical Intelligence for Success in School." *Educational Leadership,* Sept. 1990, pp. 35–39.

Tobias, S. *They're Not Dumb, They're Different: Stalking the Second Tier.* Tucson, Ariz.: Research Corporation—A Foundation for the Advancement of Science, 1990.

Tremmel, R. "Investigating Productivity and Other Factors in the Writer's Practice." *Freshman English News,* 1989, 17 (2), 19–25.

Wulff, D. H., Nyquist, J. D., and Abbott, R. D. "Students' Perceptions of Large Classes." In M. G. Weimer (ed.), *Teaching Large Classes Well.* New Directions for Teaching and Learning, no. 32. San Francisco: Jossey-Bass, 1987.

Robert Boice directs the Faculty Instructional Support Office at the State University of New York, Stony Brook, where he is also professor of psychology. His interests as a researcher and practitioner focus on faculty as colleagues, writers, and teachers.

What on earth can we academics learn from business people about how to evaluate and improve college teaching? I learned a lot.

Report on a Trip Downtown

Kenneth O. Doyle

When, in 1954, Professor Lee Cronbach originally reported on his "psychometric mission to Clinicia," he concluded that he had learned much from his visit to the Land of the Infidel (Cronbach, 1954). He had gained, for example, an appreciation of the complexity, the nonorthogonality, of the human enterprise. Thirty-eight years later, although with less insight and considerably less wit than demonstrated by Cronbach, I can report that I too have learned much from traveling in a foreign land. For the past eight years I have traveled in the Land of the Business World Downtown, where I have been financial adviser to families and family businesses on such matters as pension plans, employee benefits, investments, and insurance. The land from which I have traveled is the familiar (but not necessarily united) State of Academe, where I was for many years a differential psychologist interested in the psychometrics of evaluations. Now I am a financial psychologist interested in the psychodynamics of money.

Drawing on this past, the question I want to address in this chapter is the following: What on earth can we academics learn from business people about how to evaluate and improve college teaching? I learned a lot.

First, I learned to focus more on the recipients of my services. It does not seem to make much difference whether the recipient is someone I am trying to advise about a pension plan or someone I am trying to teach about generalizability theory: The extent to which I get my point across is a direct function of the degree to which I understand my recipient.

Salespeople practice what many teachers preach: We reach different people in different ways. I have known this intellectually all of my academic life, but I never really understood it until I tried to do it one-to-one with clients on a daily basis. If I were doing evaluation research these days, I would be looking closely at the interactions between different kinds of teachers and different kinds of students, particularly as measured by such devices as the Social Styles Inventory (Merrill and Reid, 1981) and the Myers-Briggs Type Indicator (Myers, 1980).

Second, I learned not to need to be so safe all the time. Protests notwithstanding, the tasks of evaluating and improving college teaching really are not any more difficult than those of evaluating and improving the performance of a sales manager or a consultant. The difference is that we academics are inclined to get ourselves into the paralysis of analysis, trying to pick away at everything in sight until the whole process is frozen in its tracks.

I am not advocating the use of unreliable or invalid data. To the contrary, I am advocating that we go ahead and use data that may be imperfect but are still good enough to do the job. Otherwise, we risk using data that are truly unreliable and invalid: personal impressions, hallway rumors, and gossip. If I were working in teaching evaluation and improvement these days, I would concentrate on how to use the data available.

Third, I learned about honoring social and political differences. As we rally round the flag of academic freedom, I am afraid we focus more on protecting our own jobs than on protecting minority expression. I have seen academic careers threatened because assistant professors were Catholic, because they were black, because they were capitalist, because they were socialist, because they were behaviorist, because they were humanist, because they were female, because they were male, and (even though I can understand this one) because they were psychologists. In short, their careers were threatened not because they were incompetent but because they were competent in ways that were not politically correct or were out of favor with the prevailing groups in their respective departments or colleges.

During my excursions into the business world, I truly never saw anyone try to get rid of an associate because he or she did not fit in with the majority values or because he or she (to quote a professor I recently met) "just wasn't one of us." If I worked in evaluation and development these days, I would seriously think about exploring unspoken biases and prejudices that are alive and all too well in academe, and that by their intolerance can destroy careers.

Fourth, I learned that everybody does not have to be a world-class performer in everything. Downtown, in the business world, there is a great deal of joint work done by teams of people whose skills and styles complement one another. An extroverted salesperson may join forces with an introverted technician, for instance. No one asks the back room actuary to go out and excite large groups, and no one asks the charismatic speaker to do statistical projections. Business managers, like the Golden Age Greeks, seem to know that world-class skills do not often coincide in the same person. We academics, however, ask the same person to be a charismatic public speaker, a rigorous statistician and methodologist, a warm and receptive counselor, an effective fund-raiser, a productive author, and (preserve us!) a dedicated committee worker. If I were in evaluation and development, I would study ways of capitalizing on an individual's best skills and compensating for his or her weaknesses.

Fifth, I learned the importance of civility in an organization. In the business organizations where I have worked, not everybody likes everybody else. Personalities clash, values clash, tastes clash, and people compete vigorously for reputations, popularity, jobs, money, and perks. Yet somehow they get along.

Some colleges and universities that I know seem to have more than their fair share of faculty who affront fundamental civility, who are angry all of the time, who tyrannize students, staff, and junior faculty, who calumniate and slander and backbite, who whine ceaselessly about everything under the sun, and even (sad but true) whose body odors bring tears to the eyes. In the business firms where I have worked, management would have intervened. If I were in faculty evaluation and development, I would probably let somebody else deal with these problems!

Sixth, I learned that standards for faculty performance can be preserved even under duress. I have watched business firms fire their very best producers if those firms felt that those producers did not meet high standards for quality of work or ethics. It cost the owners of those businesses a lot of money to preserve their integrity.

Yet, I know of faculty in well-respected institutions who are so incompetent in the classroom that students change majors to avoid their courses, faculty whose research simply is not worthy any more and who do not even bother to go to their offices most of the time. There are the "driftwood" faculty who just float lazily toward their pensions. If I were in the evaluation and improvement business, I would look for ways to identify and deal with perennial driftwood.

Seventh, I learned that standards for student performance can also be preserved. The problem of standards is certainly not just with driftwood faculty. People in the same firms that fire top producers who do not meet the firm's own standards also refuse to work with clients who do not care about standards. In the academy, the problem seems to be that more than a few faculty are lowering their academic standards for fear of reprisal on student evaluations. I saw two separate instances in just the past year of small groups of students banding together to "get" a professor: one because she taught content more difficult than the students wanted and the other because he gave exams that students felt were too hard. If I were doing research on evaluation and development, I would try to determine the contribution, if any, of student evaluations to what appears to be an ongoing erosion of academic standards.

Eighth, I learned important and surprising lessons about humaneness in evaluation. I do not think it is humane to open someone to the possibility of a negative evaluation without at the same time providing some meaningful help toward improvement. Business firms know how much money they have invested in their employees; they know that they waste money if they discourage or dismiss potentially productive employees and so they spend large sums of money on intensive training programs. I am appalled to see how little progress many academic institutions have made in the past twenty years toward providing effective teaching improvement services to the faculty that they evaluate.

I also do not think it is humane to drop new assistant professors into departments and expect them to sink or swim on the basis of what they learned in graduate school. I have watched business firms provide intensive training, motivation, and support to new members. I continue to be amazed both at what we expect of our new academic colleagues and at how little we give them to help them through their early years. Finally, I do not think it is humane to disregard a colleague's personal circumstances when we do an evaluation. I have watched business managers moderate their judgment (within reason) because they knew that a colleague was undergoing a personal crisis (for example, divorce). I have also watched faculty (who lay claim to a higher sensibility) always take the hard line in almost identical circumstances. It is remarkable how we academics can be so sensitive to humankind in the abstract—and so insensitive to real people.

Now, I do not want to be naive about all of this. The business firms in which I worked did some pretty dumb things too, but that is another story. These firms were also a select sample. I chose them because they were supposed to be "the best in the business," because they had the best management and the best technicians that I could find, and because they were reputed to be exceptionally cordial places to work. Moreover, I suspect that because I was "the professor," the people with whom I worked were a bit more tolerant of my eccentricities than they might otherwise have been. Therefore, I cannot conclude that the whole Business World Downtown is a better place to work than the State of Academe or that it does a better job than we do in personnel evaluation and development—only that there is a lot some of us can learn from some of them.

References

Cronbach, L. J. "Report on a Psychometric Mission to Clinicia." *Psychometrica*, 1954, *19*, 263–270.
Merrill, D. W., and Reid, R. H. *Personal Styles and Effective Performance*. Radnor, Penn.: Chilton, 1981.
Myers, E. B. *Introduction to Type*. Palo Alto, Calif.: Consulting Psychologists Press, 1980.

Kenneth O. Doyle is research associate in the Office of the Vice President for Academic Affairs, University of Minnesota, Minneapolis.

INDEX

Abbott, R. D., 118, 120
Abrami, P. C., 84, 95, 99, 102, 106, 108
Accommodators, 75
Affiliative model, of consultation, 44, 45
Aleamoni, L. M., 12, 13, 14, 17, 66, 80, 86, 91, 95
Andrews, J.D.W., 45, 48
Angelo, T. A., 32, 33, 35, 117, 120
Arizona, University of, 86
Arnold, S., 12, 18
Arreola, R. A., 86, 91, 95
Ashford, S. J., 34, 35, 39, 48
Assessment, 53, 61-62; of components of teaching, 54-55; current approach to, 53-54; and design or redesign of instruction, 58-60; and field testing and implementation, 60-61; and problem clarification, 56-58
Assimilators, 75
Axelrod, J., 12, 17

Baldwin, R., 18
Bean, T., 70, 81
Beckey, J., 9, 17, 74, 81
Bentley, R. J., 26, 36
Bergquist, W. H., 9, 10, 11, 13, 17, 74, 80
Berk, R. A., 86, 95
Bess, J. L., 12, 17
Binder, J., 12, 18
Blackburn, R. T., 102, 108
Blake, R. R., 42, 44, 45, 46, 48
Boehrer, J., 118, 120
Boice, R., 3, 100, 111, 112, 113, 114, 115, 116, 117, 120, 121
Brandenburg, D. C., 12, 18, 56, 62
Braskamp, L. A., 9, 10, 18, 26, 29, 30, 35, 36, 56, 62
Brinko, K. T., 2, 14, 18, 30, 36, 39, 40, 45, 47, 48, 49, 103, 104
Business, teaching insights from, 123-126

California, University of, 86
Cannon, W. B., 7, 17
Cappe, L., 10, 18
Carnegie Foundation: on beliefs about teaching, 26; on teaching profession, 22-24
Carrier, C. A., 42, 44, 45, 46, 48
Carroll, J. G., 16, 17, 46, 48
Cash, W. B., 42, 48
Cashin, W. E., 85, 88, 91, 95
Centra, J. A., 9, 12, 13, 17, 66, 81, 88, 91, 95, 105, 108
Clark, J., 9, 17, 74, 81
Classroom research, 117-118
Classroom Research Project, 32
Class size, and student ratings, 91
Cohen, P. A., 10, 14, 17, 39, 48, 66, 81, 84, 95, 102, 108
Coil, A., 70, 81
Cole, D. L., 114, 117, 120
Collaborative/process model, of consultation, 44, 45
Colorado, University of, 1
Comeaux, M. A., 29, 36
Confrontational model, of consultation, 44, 45-46
Consultants: and feedback, 9-10; and student ratings, 92-94; value of, 65-66
Consultation, 39; dynamics of, 46-47; and faculty self-diagnosis, 80; follow-up on, 80; models of, 42, 44-46; phases of, 40-42, 43; recommendations on, 47-48
Convergers, 75
Cooper, C. R., 41, 46, 48
Course/Instructor Evaluation Questionnaire, 86
Cranton, P. A., 3, 99, 104, 105, 108, 109
Cronbach, L. J., 123, 126
Cross, K. P., 32, 35, 117, 120
Cummings, L. L., 34, 35, 39, 48

Dalgaard, K. A., 42, 44, 45, 46, 48
d'Apollonia, S., 84, 95, 102, 108
Data: collection of, 66-67; course, curriculum, and program development, 55; for design or redesign, 60; for field testing and implementation, 61; imperfect, 124; and instructional awareness, 69-72; from inventories, 75-76; from minute papers, 76; needs and sources

Data (continued)
of, 77, 78–79; from observations, 76–77; and preconditions, 67–68; for program clarification, 57–58; from student evaluations, 72–75; for teaching improvement, 77, 80. *See also* Feedback; Information
Daugherty, M., 18
Davey, K. B., 13, 17
Davies, I. K., 14, 17, 42, 44, 48
Diamond, R. M., 55, 56, 57, 59, 62
Divergers, 75
Dixon, N. M., 76, 81
Downey, R. G., 85, 95
Doyle, K. O., 3, 100, 123, 126

Eble, K. E., 21, 35
Edington, D. W., 102, 108
Epstein, J., 21, 36
Erickson, B. L., 74, 81
Erickson, G. R., 39, 48, 74, 81
Erwin, T. D., 54, 62
Evaluation. *See* Student evaluations
Ewell, P. T., 53, 62
Exams, 70–71

Faculty: and evaluation and development, 33–34; and feedback, 34; instructional awareness among, 69–72; lack of training for, 126; and reflection on standards, 34; and skill learning, 35; on teaching beliefs and practices, 25–27; on teaching profession, 22–25. *See also* Teachers; Teaching assistants (TAs)
Faculty development: faculty-centered, 33–35; first-factor program for, 115–120
Feedback, 2, 7–8, 15; consequences of, 14–15, 16–17; and consultation, 39, 41, 43; context of, 8–9, 16; environment for discussion of, 14, 16; faculty-centered, 34; message of, 10–11, 16; recipient of, 11–13, 16; sender of, 9–10, 16. *See also* Data; Information
Feedback loop model, 27–28; faculty in, 33–35; information in, 28–31, 34; standards in, 31–32, 34; teaching repertoires in, 32–33, 35
Feldman, K. A., 84, 95, 99, 102, 108
Fink, L. D., 111, 118, 120
First-factor rule, 116; program for teaching, 115–120

Flanders, N. A., 76, 81
Fowler, D. L., 26, 29, 30, 35
Fox, D., 25, 36
Franklin, J., 3, 4, 30, 36, 72, 83, 86, 88, 89, 91, 95, 96, 102, 109
Fuhrman, B. S., 9, 17
Fuller, F. F., 14, 18

Gallessich, J., 42, 44, 46, 49
Geis, G. L., 2, 7, 11, 12, 18, 19, 28, 54, 63, 85, 103, 104
Gil, D. H., 7, 18
Glasman, N. S., 13, 18
Gmelch, W. H., 24, 36
Goldberg, S. R., 16, 17, 46, 48
Goldstein, A. P., 10, 18
Grasha, A. F., 9, 17, 46, 49
Gray, P. J., 2, 53, 55, 61, 62, 83

Halliburton, D., 18
Hiscock, P., 54, 62
Hoffmann, J., 21, 30, 36
Horowitz, S. M., 102, 108

IDEA form, 86
Information, 2–3; for improving teaching, 72–77. *See also* Data; Feedback
Instructional effectiveness. *See* Teaching effectiveness

Jackson, A. S., 115, 119, 120
Job satisfaction, and teaching effectiveness, 102–103
Johnson, G. R., 76, 81
Jung, C., 107, 108

Kanfer, F. H., 10, 18
Kansas State University, 86
Karren, R., 35, 36
Kerns, M., 69, 82
Kerr, S., 10, 18
Klos, D. M., 102, 108
Knoop, R., 3, 99, 103, 108, 109
Kolb, D. A., 75, 76, 81
Kolb Learning Styles Inventory (LSI), 75–76

Levanoni, E., 103, 108
Levinson-Rose, J., 39, 49
Lewis, K. G., 3, 65, 73, 76, 81, 82, 83
L'Hommedieu, R. L., 94, 95
Lin, Y-G., 18

Locke, E. A., 103, 107, 108
Lovrich, N. P., 24, 36
Lowther, M. M., 26, 36
Lucas, A. F., 119, 120

McGill, L. T., 28, 36
Machell, D. F., 100, 108
McKeachie, W. J., 12, 14, 18, 66, 81, 115, 120
Maehr, M. L., 26, 36
Mann, R. D., 12, 18
Manning, B. A., 14, 17
Marchese, T. J., 54, 62
Marincovich, M., 18
Marsh, H., 84, 91, 95, 99, 102, 108
Martens, G. G., 26, 36
Marx, R. D., 35, 36
Mason, E. J., 46, 47, 49
Massachusetts, University of, 86
Mathis, B. C., 18
Menges, R. J., 2, 12, 14, 15, 18, 21, 25, 27, 28, 30, 32, 36, 37, 39, 49, 66-67, 81, 94, 95, 103, 104
Merrill, D. W., 124, 126
Miami-Dade Community College, 1
Minter, R. L., 42, 48
Minute papers, 76
Moffett, M. M., 18
Mooney, C. J., 22, 23, 36
Mortensen, L., 39, 49
Motivation, and perception of feedback, 13
Mouton, J. S., 42, 44, 45, 46, 48
Munson, P. J., 46, 47, 49
Murray, H. G., 10, 18, 29, 36, 84, 86, 95
Myers, E. B., 124, 126

Neigler, C., 18
Nork, J., 18
Northeastern University, 86
Nyquist, J. D., 118, 120

Observations, data from, 76-77
O'Hanlon, J., 39, 49
Okagaki, L., 115, 119, 120
Oliver, W. F., 9, 19
Orban, D. A., 39, 40, 46, 49
Ory, J. C., 9, 10, 12, 18, 26, 29, 30, 35, 36, 56, 62, 86, 95
Oseroff-Varnell, D., 21, 30, 36

Parrett, J. L., 69, 82
Pearson, D., 103, 108
Peterson, P. L., 29, 36
Phillips, S. R., 9, 10, 11, 13, 17, 74, 80
Pieper, D. M., 12, 18
Povlacs, J. T., 32, 36, 73, 74, 81
Preparation time: decreasing, 115, 116-117; of new faculty, 112; of "quick starters," 113
Prescription model, of consultation, 42, 44, 45
President's Teaching Scholars Program, 1
Price, R. D., 39, 40, 49
Product model, of consultation, 42, 44

Questionnaires. *See* Student ratings

Rando, W. C., 12, 18, 25, 36
Readings, 70
Reid, R. H., 124, 126
Research: classroom, 117-118; on teaching effectiveness, 106-108
Rotem, A., 13, 18
Russell, T. L., 11, 18
Rutt, D. P., 10, 18, 39, 40, 42, 44, 49

Sackin, H. D., 10, 18
Sarkisian, E., 118, 120
Schein, E. H., 42, 44, 46, 49
Schwartz, F. S., 48, 49
Scriven, M., 105, 109
Seiler, R., 103, 108
Seldin, P., 9, 18, 56, 62, 100, 109
Sell, G. R., 13, 17
Shaeffer, J. M., 28, 36
Simpson, D. E., 42, 44, 45, 46, 48
Slocum, J. W., 10, 18
Small Group Instructional Diagnosis (SGID), 74-75
Smith, R., 104, 108
Smith, R. A., 48, 49
Snyder, M., 31, 36
Socialization time: increasing, 117; of "quick starters," 113
Sorcinelli, M. D., 100, 109
Standards, 31-32; faculty-centered reflection on, 34
Stark, J. S., 26, 36
Sternberg, R. J., 115, 119, 120
Stevens, E., 31, 32, 33, 36, 103, 109
Stevens, J. J., 12, 13, 14, 17

Student Evaluation of Educational Quality form, 86
Student evaluations: faculty view of, 21; and lowering of academic standards, 125; from midsemester feedback, 73–75; from previous semesters/quarters, 72–73. *See also* Student ratings
Student ratings, 83–84, 94–95; analyses and reports of, 88–89; and consultant, 92–94; faculty perception of, 29–31; interpretation of, 89–92; questionnaire items for, 85; technical considerations for, 86–87; wording for, 87; written comments on, 87–88. *See also* Student evaluations
Sudweeks, R., 56, 62
Svinicki, M. D., 18, 76, 81
Sweeney, J. M., 46, 49
Syllabus, 70
Szego, C. K., 118, 120

Taylor-Way, D., 69, 81
Teacher-Course Evaluation Project Questionnaire, 86
Teachers: exploring preconditions with, 67–68; new faculty as, 111–113; "quick starters" as, 113–115; as recipients of feedback, 11–13, 16; slower starters as, 115–120. *See also* Faculty; Teaching assistants (TAs)
Teaching, 3–4; assessing components of, 54–55; beliefs and practices in, 25–27; data for improvement of, 77, 80; dimensions and behaviors of, 84–85; faculty-centered evaluation and development in, 33–35; feedback about, 7–17; feedback loop model of, 27–33; first-factor rule in, 116; good, 66, 91; insights from business on, 123–126; as profession, 22–25; and teaching effectiveness model, 103–108

Teaching Analysis by Students (TABS) form, 74, 86
Teaching assistants (TAs): feedback for, 28–29; meaning of teaching for, 25; training of, 118
Teaching effectiveness, 99–100; and decisions about teaching, 105–106; and improving teaching, 103–105; and job satisfaction, 102–103; model of, 100–102; research on, 106–108
Teaching Goals Inventory, 32
Teaching-Learning Project, of Miami-Dade Community College, 1
Terenzini, P. T., 53, 62
Textbooks, 70
Theall, M., 3, 4, 30, 36, 72, 83, 86, 88, 89, 91, 95, 96, 102, 109
Tiberius, R. G., 10, 12, 18, 31, 37, 75, 81
Tilles, S., 42, 44, 46, 49
Tobias, S., 76, 82, 119, 120
Tosti, D. T., 11, 19
Tremmel, R., 114, 120
Tuckman, B. W., 9, 19

Videotape, 10, 16, 29, 69

Walton, J. M., 35, 37
Walz, M., 18
Watts, L., 15, 19
Weimer, M., 67, 68, 69, 82
Wergin, J. F., 46, 47, 49
White, E. M., 53, 62
Wiener, N., 7, 19
Wieties, R., 86, 95
Wilke, P. K., 24, 36
Wilson, R., 76, 82
Writing: increasing, 115, 117; of "quick starters," 113–115
Written comments analysis grid, 73
Wulff, D. H., 118, 120

Ordering Information

NEW DIRECTIONS FOR TEACHING AND LEARNING is a series of paperback books that presents ideas and techniques for improving college teaching, based both on the practical expertise of seasoned instructors and on the latest research findings of educational and psychological researchers. Books in the series are published quarterly in Fall, Winter, Spring, and Summer and are available for purchase by subscription as well as by single copy.

SUBSCRIPTIONS for 1991 cost $45.00 for individuals (a savings of 20 percent over single-copy prices) and $60.00 for institutions, agencies, and libraries. Please do not send institutional checks for personal subscriptions. Standing orders are accepted.

SINGLE COPIES cost $14.95 when payment accompanies order. (California, New Jersey, New York, and Washington, D.C., residents please include appropriate sales tax.) Billed orders will be charged postage and handling.

DISCOUNTS FOR QUANTITY ORDERS are available. Please write to the address below for information.

ALL ORDERS must include either the name of an individual or an official purchase order number. Please submit your order as follows:
  Subscriptions: specify series and year subscription is to begin
  Single copies: include individual title code (such as TL1)

MAIL ALL ORDERS TO:
  Jossey-Bass Inc., Publishers
  350 Sansome Street
  San Francisco, California 94104

FOR SALES OUTSIDE OF THE UNITED STATES CONTACT:
  Maxwell Macmillan International Publishing Group
  866 Third Avenue
  New York, New York 10022

OTHER TITLES AVAILABLE IN THE
NEW DIRECTIONS FOR TEACHING AND LEARNING SERIES
Robert J. Menges, Editor-in-Chief
Marilla D. Svinicki, Associate Editor

TL47 Applying the Seven Principles for Good Practice in Undergraduate Education, *Arthur W. Chickering, Zelda F. Gamson*
TL46 Classroom Research: Early Lessons from Success, *Thomas A. Angelo*
TL45 College Teaching: From Theory to Practice, *Robert J. Menges, Marilla D. Svinicki*
TL44 Excellent Teaching in a Changing Academy: Essays in Honor of Kenneth Eble, *Feroza Jussawalla*
TL43 Student Ratings of Instruction: Issues for Improving Practice, *Michael Theall, Jennifer Franklin*
TL42 The Changing Face of College Teaching, *Marilla D. Svinicki*
TL41 Learning Communities: Creating Connections Among Students, Faculty, and Disciplines, *Faith Gabelnick, Jean MacGregor, Roberta S. Matthews, Barbara Leigh Smith*
TL40 Integrating Liberal Learning and Professional Education, *Robert A. Armour, Barbara S. Fuhrmann*
TL39 Teaching Assistant Training in the 1990s, *Jody D. Nyquist, Robert D. Abbott*
TL38 Promoting Inquiry in Undergraduate Learning, *Frederick Stirton Weaver*
TL37 The Department Chairperson's Role in Enhancing College Teaching, *Ann F. Lucas*
TL36 Strengthening Programs for Writing Across the Curriculum, *Susan H. McLeod*
TL35 Knowing and Doing: Learning Through Experience, *Pat Hutchings, Allen Wutzdorff*
TL34 Assessing Students' Learning, *Robert E. Young, Kenneth E. Eble*
TL33 College Teaching and Learning: Preparing for New Commitments, *Robert E. Young, Kenneth E. Eble*
TL32 Teaching Large Classes Well, *Maryellen Gleason Weimer*
TL31 Techniques for Evaluating and Improving Instruction, *Lawrence M. Aleamoni*
TL30 Developing Critical Thinking and Problem-Solving Abilities, *James E. Stice*
TL29 Coping with Faculty Stress, *Peter Seldin*
TL28 Distinguished Teachers on Effective Teaching, *Peter G. Beidler*
TL27 Improving Teacher Education, *Eva C. Galambos*
TL26 Communicating in College Classrooms, *Jean M. Civikly*
TL25 Fostering Academic Excellence Through Honors Programs, *Paul G. Friedman, Reva Jenkins-Friedman*
TL24 College-School Collaboration: Appraising the Major Approaches, *William T. Daly*
TL23 Using Research to Improve Teaching, *Janet G. Donald, Arthur M. Sullivan*
TL22 Strengthening the Teaching Assistant Faculty, *John D. W. Andrews*
TL21 Teaching as Though Students Mattered, *Joseph Katz*
TL14 Learning in Groups, *Clark Bouton, Russell Y. Garth*
TL12 Teaching Writing in All Disciplines, *C. Williams Griffin*
TL3 Fostering Critical Thinking, *Robert E. Young*
TL2 Learning, Cognition, and College Teaching, *Wilbert J. McKeachie*
TL1 Improving Teaching Styles, *Kenneth E. Eble*